I0766369

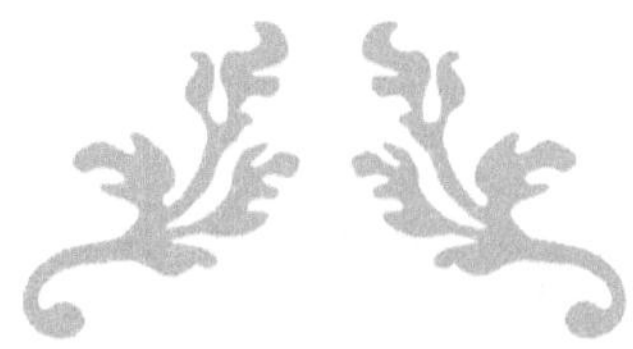

FREUD'S FALLACY

Baby Hans ~ Care~fully

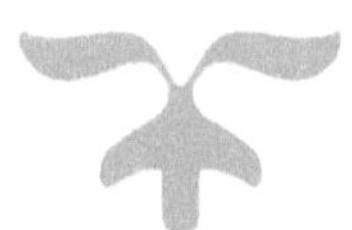

FREUD'S FALLACY

~

Baby Hans, Care~fully.

((*An Analysis*))

By

Dr Clifford Brickman

In Conjunction with

Rabbi Jay Brickman

~

2

© Copyright 2019
5780

A Little Child Shall Lead Them.

. . .

*Did you know .. Sigmund Freud called young **Hans** a "young <u>**Degenerate**</u>" ?*

.. Quoting Freud (SF:),

" *... it would be illegitimate therefore to apply to other normal children, conclusions, which might perhaps be true of him (Hans) .. "*

(((Well this is a good Ear-catching phrase to begin.)))

We *will* let you know dear reader,

Who we are & where we are, What this all means; and show you a little bit, how, we study these things in *great detail* here ~ I think more than almost anybody has, because ..

- Who has the knowledge & patience to *really* go through things .. especially during these days with short attention spans .. all these *details* .. such as *you* and also *me?* - in terms of our backgrounds & what we're *good* at looking *at* ..

<u>Overview</u>.

First please allow us to give you an overview and a bit of background, to that very first characterization by Freud on **Hans** *and his* **'deviance.'**

We are right now closely reviewing **Little Hans** in Sigmund Freud's Volume *X (Ten)* first half of his volume that he titles, "*Little Hans*" pages 1 to 150.

His volume ten is from the year *1909* of his 24 Volumes written 1886 to 1938. *"Little Hans"* is Sigmund Freud's

-1st Case History-

Written & put together to support, to prove Freud's theories.

We're currently on page 101 about to move into *Part III "The Discussion"* by **Sigmund Freud**.

We have spent many months, a hundred pages on a*ll these details* covering little Hans - or as I prefer.. your *(JB)* calling him, *"Baby Hans"* which I like even better.

.. and so in his *Discussion* section which we can get to I think he's doing a *"what-if"* in some ways. He's coming up with people who are going to *object* to his ideas and theories thus far - in his Discussion of a hundred pages of baby Hans. So he's coming up with, like a good lawyer might, talking about the "Other point of view" (basically to undermine it).

On the other hand Freud himself is referring to little Hans as a *"little degenerate"* and as I said to you, is that tongue in cheek ..

What do you think .. ?

JB: No, I don't think so ...
   It doesn't *sound* like it's tongue-in-cheek.

CB: I'm not sure how I would describe that in literary terms. He is bringing up a point of view that he is trying to promote which is, little kids - and human beings generally - have a lot of *"Polymorphous Perverse,"* maybe at their *Core,* he might believe.

JB: He (Freud) says, *"This may not apply to other, normal children, conclusions which might perhaps be true of him."*

This is an *abnormal* child. I don't think he's saying that *all* children are this.

Side-note from CB. .. True that Hans was not the usual child of his generation with the Authoritarian approach of his time. The normal child would be brow-beaten, emotionally repressed, socially suppressed, and with cultural support, even admiration, for doing so.

CB: Well . oh, uh .. so you're saying *he's* saying this is an *abnormal* child .. *?*

JB: Yeah!

CB: Well what do *you* think about that?

JB: .. *he doesn't sound like that to me ..*
   He seems like a *normal* kid to me.
      ((Mutual chuckles .. & laughter.))

CB: So it's interesting how these past .. I don't know, it's almost six months ,, you and I see it almost *exactly* the same. When we really start looking at *the details!*

In fact, that, Little *Hans* seems to be more normal than the *adults!* He stands up for things that don't make sense when he hears them! He doesn't accept the idea that a *stork (* lol *)* delivered a child! -Well he *"accepts"* it but he doesn't *buy* it! ..he gets confused by this.

And many other things.

- Or when *Theory* is kind of *pushed* on him. They call it *Enlightenment* … "when *We ENLIGHTEN* Little Hans..*!*"

JB: Um-hymm*! ah-ha!*

CB: And, and when I say "<u>we</u>" there's <u>two</u> 'psychoanalysts' involved, as you and I know. One is Freud, and the other is.. *{ I was going to say "Freud's father" - interesting Freudian slip }*

..Freud's *follower -I.e.,* Little *Hans'* **father**..

JB: -Was he a psychoanalyst also?

CB: -I don't think so. I don't know if he psychoanalyzed *anybody else* actually. I'd like to look into that .. But he performed ..he was like a psychoanalyst *in training..*

JB: Oh is *that right?!*

CB: Something like that .. I'd like to really pin that one down because he's the one who reached out to Freud; he said, "I really like your theories.." Excetera excetera. And this was the time In Freud's presentation development, the people were saying, "Okay, now *prove your theories!*"

So little Hans' papa and mother offered their son, their baby, as a good test case*!*   JB: Um-hymm.   *CB:* And both of them I think were in therapy with Freud or came to know Freud..

And they were..kind of pushing Freud's.. Or not necessarily pushing *that they were aware of ..* I think they *were* pushing on little Hans.

JB: I -I didn't get that the *mother* was in therapy ..

CB: Yeah she *too* .. had some kind of *relationship* with Freud .. *JB:* hymm! *CB:* Both of those I think we have to pin down historically. But as you and I would say, there's a lot of question to this.

And I think Freud will say in the next paragraph, what the questions are .. *you know* same questions *we've* had now for a 100 pages over *6 months!*

So Freud brings up the *"other side"* of the issue, in *some* ways agreeing with what we're saying. But I think he's then going to try to *umm rationalize,* why that's *not so!*

JB: We should read this "Discussion" together I think.

CB: Ok. I was going to suggest we hold off on it .. and Summarize what we've come up with already, but okay that's okay.. Yeah, why don't we. People can see how we get into this *as* we're doing it!

And then later we can go back into more detail .. I have a tremendous amount of notes from the last hundred pages, and thoughts on what "Enlightenment" means.

..*you know* from the Outside-*in*. I think that *some* psychoanalysts may think *that*, "Okay..we enlighten the patient with *our theories!*"

I think that's..you and I would agree I think, that's wrong. The enlightenment should be from the inside-out, no?

JB: w-e-l-l … I-I I think it's a *joint process* .. I mean, I think that each has some contribution.

CB: Well I think that a number of psychoanalysts, would say that - that we each have a contribution. I got into a discussion with Dr. Galatzer-Levy when I first started (in a reading group). My position was it should be kind of *more* from the patient, maybe a cooperative endeavor, and his point I think, at that point was, well maybe some comes *more* from the psychoanalyst.

But you know, *that* needs to be really flushed out, a *lot.* That's *to me, that's* .. a *Vital Distinction* - what "**Enlightenment**" means - and does it come from the Outside-*in* or from the *Inside*-out?

JB: R-i-g-h-t.

CB: So, you were pretty committed to Freudian analysis for many years. *JB:* right! *CB:* Should we tell them you've also became a Jungian as well or no? *JB: sure* .. sure. (*lol*)

JB: But I don't see a conflict you know. I.. I see Jung's theories as sort of being *layered on top* of Freud's. I don't think they're contradictory. I think they just supplement it.

CB: Well yeah you never thought that there was any disagreement between them. I always thought their- One of their big fights was over the phrase, *"I want to keep my Authority."*

- is what Freud was saying - and Jung seriously, strenuously objected*!* That was part of their big split*!*

- but I know you haven't run into that or hadn't thought of that so, you know we've had different points of view on a lot of this over decades.

What's interesting is, you were trained in this by going through it for how many years, at five times a week?

JB: I think three, three-and-a-half years. *CB:* ok, at four or five times a week? *JB: yes - five! CB: five.*

CB: And then I went to your same analyst when I was a kid for maybe 10 months I would say..when I was eleven, ten or eleven. *JB:* um-hymm

CB: I thought it was a very supportive experience. Never *felt* he was pushing anything on me..but what do I know?

Maybe..maybe there was something happening that I was not aware of..all these years later.   (*8 min 18 sec*)

JB: .. no I don't think he was a pushy..analyst. I think he was mostly, listening.

CB: I think the things we're looking at with Freud, you'll find a lot different from *uh*..Dr. John Thurrott of many years ago.

CB: And then, to mention what I alluded to earlier: I've been a therapist In many areas from let's say 1970. *Family* therapy. *Hypno*therapy. Neo-Freudian therapy.

~ and then over three decades..have developed my own point of view in terms of the *Inner Core & the Still Soft Voice -more on SSV later-*

And, at U of Chicago we really did a lot of process recording looking at things..in depth.

With *your* background, how long have you been doing the Bible study?

JB: Oh I would say .. probably started..around 1950
    / *CB:* ..yeah I was going to say in '55 in Milwaukee /
    .. Well in Staten Island, maybe in 1950 ..

CB: Yeah well that makes sense, since really 1950. And I think one of your groups Is now completing a reading and group discussion of the *whole Bible!*
It took.. let's see, 50 .. 70 years?!

JB: .. *We*'re in the Book of *Proverbs.*
  CB: Proverbs! .. but you went through the *whole Bible!*
    JB: yes
  CB: Well that's almost 70 years .. And then your other group meets on Shabbat. You go through the Five Books of Moses, what? every seven or eight years.

JB: Right.

CB: Takes 7 or 8 years*!* I've alluded to Dr Galatzer-Levy's [reading] group at the Chicago Psychoanalytic Institute. I think his group as far as I know has been going 10 years to cover so far 10 volumes of Freud.

JB: Hymm!

CB: So how many people have the capacity, the depth or the *patience-* *(mutual laughter)* *JB: yeah .. patience!* -to look at these things*?!* *.. yeah!*

So I've found: Surprisingly, maybe not so surprising, when it's just you and me going through this, I think it's even more intense and really gets to the point.

I've been in your [study] group and it's always interesting and fascinating, and you have Conservative-wing and Radical Left-wing / Right wing, all sorts of interesting *Conflicts* and *ideas.*

.. and also *Divergences.* So when it's really just you and me looking at this, I think it's even easier to focus on this..what's being said and how we look at it.

JB: Exactly.

CB: It's very *entertaining* when you have a whole bunch of people with all sorts of ideas.. Knowledgeable, not-so-knowledgeable, fanciful whatever ..

But this has been *great!* We've covered a hundred pages in I'd say about 6 months*!* *[plus].* And we're doing it more than weekly - - sometimes three-times-a-week or more.

JB: yes. Um-hym!

CB: And since the psychoanalytic group meets one time a month on this I think we are getting into more detail than they would be doing, or are *able* to be doing.

JB: I would think so!

CB: So *okay!* Should we move on to where are we on that page? Maybe we'll spend a few minutes on how we *look* at these things ..

Page 101

JB: .. yeah, we're close to the bottom of page 101.
11 min 35 sec yeah and he says, Because he.. *(SF:)*

".. was a young 'degenerate'; it would be illegitimate, therefore, to apply to other, normal children conclusions which might perhaps be true of him."

JB: So he [Freud] is making a distinction between Hans who is a *sick* kid and *normal* children - who don't respond that way.

CB: Oh I see; yeah.

-I think he's doing partly, *"what if?"* and partly, yeah, a "degenerate," he's talking for the public; *they* think he's a *degenerate* for what reason*?*

.. "Neurosis" .. "Degenerate" ..

JB: .. *no* I think that *Freud* thinks he's a degenerate*!* ..

CB: .. well *(Slight chuckle) umm* .. I- I might be *almost* as tough on Freud as you on that one. Because earlier in the hundred Pages he was getting to that *idea..*

I do think that he both admires litt——le Hans as being a little *Explorer*, but yeah-he d*oes* use that word "<u>*degenerate*</u>" here. Like--where does *that* come from?
JB: **Pow-**

JB: **Powerful word!**

CB: **Yeah.** And as you & I have discussed - we do this in studying the Bible too- What'show do we look at it in Hebrew or in other languages Or other interpretations? So this is the *English* word ..

JB: ..and you were going to check that out you said..

CB: -yeah at some point when I figure out how to collate German and the English; trying to get a better method of doing that through the computer. So I guess we'll be stuck with looking at it from the English point of view for now.

- Don't forget, Anna Freud was part of the translation process as well as was a good friend of Freud's; and that's the word *they're* using here.

Can you continue on, about not applying that necessarily to *normal* children..
12 min 19 sec

JB: yeah, (*SF:*)

"I shall postpone consideration of this Objection since it only limits the value of the observation and does not completely nullify it."

CB: So he's..   JB: Learn a little bit something from this but not too much.

CB: So he's calling this "an Objection."

I'm thinking of this in Sales. You know your father knew about that; your daughter; I understand something of that.

When an *objection* comes up or in Psychology, *resistance* of some type .. in Sales, the idea is to *overcome* the objection. ~ Have you heard of that..type of thing?

JB: Sure*!*

CB: So I think that's what he's going to try to do here
in the next paragraph. ..That's my Prediction.

Because that's where I think he's going in this page 101 'Discussion' of what we've covered so far.

So shall we continue..see where he *goes* with this?

JB: yeah

"According to the second and more uncompromising objection, an Analysis of a child conducted by his <u>father</u> who went to work instilled with <u>my</u> theoretical views and infected with <u>my</u> prejudices .." (lol)

JB: (incredulously) -that's *Freud* speaking?!-
   CB: Yeah!

JB: He calls those views, *prejudices! ..*

".. must be entirely devoid of any objective worth .."

CB: That's funny*!* 'cause that's what I've been saying ..

JB: -Other people might be thinking-
             but that's not the case.

CB: Yeah- yeah. he's saying that's not the
case.   *umm -*
But that *is* what *you and I* have been thinkin' *!!*
-

   (*my lol*)
    -for the 100 pages- *(my laughing)*

* In terms of how they went about the
   details, Of the *Castration complex,* Of the
   so-called *Neurosis,* which I believe was
   simply a *Post-traumatic stress* reaction to
   a *Horse* falling.

JB: Yeah..!

CB: umm .. They didn't know about *PTSD*
back then; and they didn't know ..*Children..*
very well back then either in early 1900s.

So we'll continue. I felt *this paragraph* 'cause
we last looked at it on June sixteen *[2019]* .. I

thought this was the first time that Freud is *agreeing* with *everything* we have been saying.

-But he's bringing it up as an Objec(tion)-
-People *objecting* to these things.-

Should we continue with what these Objections *are*?

JB: yeah.

"A child, it will be said, is necessarily <u>highly suggestible</u>. And in regard to no one but perhaps his own father, he will allow <u>anything</u> to be forced upon him, out of gratitude to his father for taking so much notice of him."

CB: - taking so much <u>notice</u> of him -

JB: yeah.

.. "None of his assertions can have any evidential value. And everything he produces in the way of associations, fantasies and

dreams, will naturally take the direction to which they are being urged by every possible means."

JB: Well I don't get the feeling that Hans was that much pushed around by the father. I think he cared- pretty much up to his *own* ideas.

CB: Well yeah that was a *p-l-u-s* that Freud helped get going. -No I don't think he was forced by the father -but I think he was *encouraged* by the father. I would look at it as an Attachment situation even a *Hypnotic* situation.

..that he might want to *please* his father. But he's not, he's not going to put up with being *forced*. In fact he [Hans] would always come up with (*lol*) some *Really good* statements!

CB: -continuing- -which we can get into, in that first hundred pages. We both kind of admired his ..his clarity! -as a <u>*five*</u> year old -or a <u>*four*</u>-year-old especially!

JB: Good*!* Right*!*   *So uh ..*

"Once more in short the whole thing is simply Suggestion."
  - S.F.

JB: I don't know what he means by that -

".. The only difference that in the case of a Child it {suggestion} can be unmasked much more easily than in that of an Adult."

CB: Well here's what he means by *"Suggestion."* He was trained -actually his first training- was in *Hypnosis*.

> And the whole idea of the couch was to help with the hypnosis. Because he wasn't that good at doing hypnosis, and putting people at ease. And then he realized, well maybe the couch is another way of getting into the *sleep* state.

So he knew about *Suggestion* and the hypnotic definition of "suggestion." In fact that was the hypnosis going-*on* at the time. As far as I know there was **only** *Suggestion-hypnosis* or to put it *stronger, Authoritarian-hypnosis!*

But anyway he's saying, no this *wasn't* the case!

So shall we continue with that next .. I think that's what Freud is saying, to say, 'Oh no*!* you can't put it all on *that*   {I.e., *Suggestion*} !

JB: yeah.

CB: So shall we continue with that next ..?

JB: (*SF:*)

"A singular thing. I can remember, when I first began to meddle in the conflict of scientific opinions twenty-two years ago with what derision the older generation of neurologists and psychiatrists of those days received assertions about suggestion and its effects."

CB: Oh, yeah, that's ..was his *training!* .. Well *ya ep This* is a *brand new* sentence. I've never looked at this before*!*

It's fascinating.

When he began "*to meddle ..*" in the conflict of scientific opinions .. And I -I think he's..*partly* that's a tongue-in-cheek thing, *meddle* - or some type of off-hand attempt at humor ..

Do you think he's perfectly serious when he uses that word, *meddle*? …What do *you think* he means?

JB: Let's see …
"*..when I first began to meddle in the conflict of scientific opinion ..*"

I think he's just putting himself down a little bit.

CB: Yeah …maybe in a somewhat humorous way..*?*

JB: Yeah. I think so.

CB: ..humorous for him, anyway..
   -I'll put a little smiley face next to that one-

Umm .. But he is getting into this idea of where his *Beginnings* were -as a Neurologist- as to their point of view on "Suggestion" -

Should I-we read a couple of more sentences and then stop..because so far it's going to be about 25 minutes - - and how many people are even going to stick with us for *25 minutes* let alone six months, I don't know.   *(-laughter-)*

JB: (*SF:*)

*"Since then the situation has fundamentally changed. The former aversion has been converted into an only too ready acceptance; and this has happened not only as a consequence of the impression which the work of **Liebeault and Bernheim** and their pupils could not fail to create in the course of these two decades, but also because it has since been discovered how great an economy of*

thought can be effected by the use of the catchword, "Suggestion."

((For very useful information - - look up on Internet
Liebeault and Bernheim
*   and the **Nancy** School.))*

JB: I don't know what he's talking about here, do you?

CB: Well again it's his hypnotic training. I know you were cautioned, don't get into hypnosis by that Intro Psychology person (in college) I asked you about a couple weeks ago,
        "Never use hypnosis!"   [he advised]

Studiers of Freud never get into hypnosis partly because of this bad rap about hypnosis 50 years ago. It was a justifiable rap, in terms of Authoritarianism, but we'll skip that for now.

So you're saying, what does he mean by suggestion here?

JB: Right   (*SF:*)

"Nobody knows and nobody cares what suggestion is, where it comes from, or when it arises,--*It is enough that everything* **awkward** *in the region of psychology can be labeled 'suggestion.'*

I don't know what he means by that.
        (((*SEE:* **CB ~ SSV Note** @ *Conclusion of This Section*)))

JB: (..continuing with Freud's paragraph..) (SF:)

"I do not share the view which is at present fashionable that is assertions made by children are invariably arbitrary and trustworthy."

Well ,, Of *course* he doesn't.   (*my chuckling*)

CB: You and I would agree with *that.*

CB: Because little Hans comes across as more adult than the adults in the room ~ when you look at the first hundred pages.

He's truly kind of *remarkable!* *JB: Yeah !!* ..

when we really look at the *data* and the *full detail* that's presented .. *!*

JB: We could do the article of -Reverse it- and say,
Little <u>Hans</u> is the therapist.

JB & CB: *(Laughing)*

CB: *I think* **so** *!!*   *JB:* *(chuckling)*   *(lol)*

CB: *"Following the children .."* isn't there a *Bible verse* on that?

JB: .. somethin' like that .. *(laughing)*

CB: I don't know if that's ours? .. theirs?
                - New or Old? -
      .. But .. a *children shall ..* *"a Child shall lead"* .. ?

JB: *"A little child shall lead them."*
                (more seriously put)   *Yeah ..*

CB: Is that Christian or Jewish? ..
          I don't recall where that comes from
              .. or *both*?

JB: I'll check it out if you want.

CB: *Okay*, maybe we should .. Conclude on, on
this one .. & should we stop at this point? It will
wet their whistle, of people, I think …

JB: I'll look it up. I'll get the .. I'll get them.

CB: I'll put it on Hold. .. You were saying
                          it's some type of - *what* .. ?

JB: It's a messianic-
        CB: -prediction ..   *(?)*

CB: Ok I'll put it back on Hold while you look it
up.

~

CB: So you have Isaiah, because that's what I
have on the top of the Google search too.

JB: "The Wolf also shall dwell with the Lamb."

This is a messianic prediction.

"And the Leopard shall lie down with the Kid.
And the Calf and the young Lion and the Fatling together.

"And a little Child Shall Lead Them."

~

CB: Wow, I didn't know that the *"Little child shall lead them"* came from *there.*

JB: Yeah isn't that *n i c e?!*

CB: Yeah. I knew about the *other part* of the quote .. So maybe *uh* little Hans is partly involved in this if we take all that stuff very very seriously.

JB: Y e a h !!

CB: So ..   (lol)

~

CB: Okay so shall we stop at that point?!

JB: Okay yeah.
.. I got to take a pee anyhow ..

CB: Okay. *I'll leave* that on the tape .. because that's part of all of us guys as we get over 40 or 50 ...

JB: Oh *(laughing)* okay.

CB: .. *or* 60 or 70.   Am doing some research . . .
.. *or* 80.   .. Or 90.

So okay. Well *thanks, it's been great* ..again.

JB: Yeah! *.. same here.*

CB: Ok talk to you soon

JB: *Ok bye.*   *CB:* *bye bye*

~

= *CB Note on the SSV* =

* Please take Another Look *at* the **Bold** *as* added - *at* something *hidden away* - among the multiple Sigmund Freud statements - that were customarily highly *squeezed* into each paragraph,

"Nobody knows and nobody cares where suggestion comes from, or when it arises."

((*Eureka & shazam.*)) Just realized *1:36 a.m. Wed. Aug 7 2019* that I *do* know one person who **does care** about this. *CB's* long and fruitful journey was based perhaps *primarily* upon a crucial question * that Sigmund Freud neglected - or wished to avoid, thus blocking himself, and others, from a Clinical or Theoretical Inquiry into it.

My Own Basic Question, 1985 – 1989, as described in my book,

       * **What** *is "It" and* **Where** *does "It"* **come from?**

Thanks are due to Sigmund Freud I suppose for neglecting this crucial question, and leaving it for me to pursue since 1989; the sooner many more people read about & delve into it, the better it will be for all.

You can read or hear all about my Investigation into *that specific Question* via books, e-book, Audible on amazon:

Dr Clifford Brickman, The Still Soft Voice, Breaking through to the Inner Core of Consciousness. *I.e., an Organic* **Deep Self**.

-CB

~

Our INTRO to Part 111

We're recording on August 19th 2019. The reader has read or heard our initial Introduction where we cover a number of general things about Little Hans and some specifics.

I do want to say, to all who want to actually look at the book, you can perhaps purchase or get on loan Volume 10 out of all of Freud's 20 volumes. It's the first half of Vol.10 page 1-150. *["Little Hans"]*

Or Online you can request certain page numbers. We will give a pretty good description of the quotes of which we are reviewing. But if you really want to see exactly how it's all written, you can also do that.

I'd like to introduce us a bit more in terms of our background doing counseling and therapy. We've already spoken about how we look into things more deeply - you *(JB)* in the Bible studies as well as psychology - Freud, and Jung .. I hadn't said much about me *(CB)* studying my own work for about 20 years 1989 through 2010. I was studying and re-studying my first *24 cases* in my research (*-with the organic, Deep Self-*).

So, what about you *(JB)*. In terms of counseling.. and rabbinic counseling ... ?

JB: Well, yeah, I … my entire career as a rabbi I've done quite a bit of counseling.. part of the relationship with the congregation.

CB: Would you say some of it revolves around Freudian Concepts ... or *not*.

JB: Well *most* of the congregational things are on a more superficial level, so we don't get right down onto things that happened in infancy .. which is where .. is the major source of Freud's ideas .. I wouldn't say that it has too much to do with *that*..

CB: Okay. …but working with people from half a century .. or *more*..

JB: Yeah*!* right*!* ... I also worked in counseling as a volunteer in a Counseling Center in downtown Milwaukee for a number of years too *(10 yrs),* working with people about problems they had, and were struggling with.

CB: So between you and me we have, I'd say, a hundred years or more .. *?!*

JB: Hym-hymm*!* ~ pretty *good!*

CB: .. and then one thing I should say is, my original connection with Freud was really more modern Freudian or *"Neo-freudian"* .. which I can explain in a minute ..

as well as *Transactional Analysis* which was actually a derivation of the more strict (Freudian) psychoanalysis.

((*SEE:* "**Neo-freudianism**" *-and-* "***Transactional Analysis****.*"))

~

So would you say … how would you relate to Freud as an adherent or a fan or as someone you really look *up* to?

JB: Yeah! I think he *revolutionized* the whole idea of psychology .. And I think that his *uh* basic principles are still valid *today,* and I think that a good therapist today has got to be very well acquainted with *uh* Freud and his teachings*!*

CB: Well, okay.
So I was .. in my case, a more modernized version, called "neo-freudian," where we actually look at not just what's going on in the unconscious as defined by Freud, but

also look at the social level, the family level, and we're not closed to that at all*!*

That's a level I don't think Freud really looked at very closely; I don't if they even had family therapy back in his time. Because, as we say in the field, if you work with a hundred families, and then you start seeing things a little differently in terms of whole *social* influence and milieu ..

JB: Yeah, and of course it has to do with *how deep* the therapy is, you know, I think normally when you're dealing with a person's problem and social situation, you're.. you're dealing with a person's *normal situation;* where in a psycho*analysis,* which I did experience myself, where you're going five times a week over a period of three or four *years*, then you, you have an opportunity to delve a lot more deeply .. and then you .. get into the depths of the psyche .. you get into the very infantile happenings;

and that's where Freud's great contribution *is* - in all the things that happened.

CB: Now, mostly with your*self*.. you're saying..
JB: .. for years, yeah.

CB: Mostly with your own analysis, your Freudian analysis..
JB: .. yeah, right.

CB: Now I *have worked* with *hundreds* .. hundreds of people in terms of going deep, more quickly, you'know not waiting for it to come through the intellect, but actually what Jung might call through "active imagination" - which, might be more palatable, to you.. - but I would call "imagery" and even "deep hypnosis," where you can really track down some very *early "messages,"* find out where they come from, what they are, and actually work on, being more *aware* and *changing* them.

It's called the **Family Script** .. that's **in the head**..!

So, *all of this* was a *derivation* .. *from* ..
Sigmund Freud*!* ..
.. from analysts who weren't happy with
some of the *slow* parts of the process ..

CB: .. and then you know Jerry White ..
right?
JB: yes.

CB: He's one of the "biggies" in the field of
Transactional Analysis - - Script Work .. he
would work on that. Actually he's the one
who taught me that aspect of how to do
that, *many* years ago, *before* I even knew
he was from Staten Island and was my
Sunday school teacher when I was 5..
a rather remarkable a coincidence ..

CB: So, I've had a lot of experience in that
part of it.

-But you still have a strong *Adherence..* to Freud -?- ..
JB: Yes.

CB: And you see him as "the *father*" of Psychology -?- ..
JB: Yes. Yes*!*

CB: .. because we've talked about that a little bit ..
I see him as a *pioneer* / *JB:* um-hymm / in psychology, and, I see myself as a *pioneer* in some of the work that I do.

-but I don't feel that *Pioneers* are infallible .. that .. they still have to *prove* their point and ..
JB: *I agree,* with that.

CB: So even though we have done a 100 pages now, of Little Hans, directly, and we happen to be very much *agree* on that, we *don't* think the point has been proven*!*

-but you still have a lot of *hope* that we *will get to* that point; maybe, there are other cases or maybe in the *next* 50 pages, do you think that he'll prove his *point for,* for Little Hans? ..or..or *not.*

JB: Well I *don't think* through *Little Hans! ..* I don't think.

In the first place, I don't think that he, that Freud actually *saw* him; I think these were reports from *the father?* of Little Hans *to* Freud? I don't think that he did, that he did an analysis *with the youngster.*

CB: Well he met with little Hans actually once, or twice.
There's a *great picture* on the internet of little Hans looking very stiff .. sitting on Freud's *I guess,* lap! .. 'cause Hans's legs are outstretched; Hans has a very *mature-looking* face for a three or four year old .. but he doesn't look *real comfortable (laugh) sitting on* Sigmund Freud's lap ..

((Look up photo, Sigmund Freud with Little Hans))

So you're right, he didn't do the analysis but at that time he felt that the *father* was doing the analysis. And even *Freud* brings up the ..

JB: ..That presents certain difficulties in itself *y'know*.
(8:38)

CB: .. well even Freud brings up the objection, that a lot of people are saying, exactly what *you're* saying, and I'm saying, that Little Hans could be first of all, *influenced* - because the father *followed* Freud - and so did the mother!

~

He followed, and he wanted to help prove, his theories.

~

But what you and I see, well he hasn't *proven* these theories, *not in the first hundred pages* of little Hans.

JB: - not so far -

CB: .. but you're hopeful that, "maybe another case?"
'Cuz as you say, the second part of this book is on the *Ratman* which, as Freud acknowledges, is more complicated to prove these things .. without the innocence of a little child, who is more simple and easier to *pin down.*

But one of the objections is, and Freud even mentions, is that there's going to be an *influence* .. an *influence* .. of the father *on* the son.

And I call that - it's kind of related to *hypnotic* influence, or *"suggestion."* Because Freud talked about *Suggestion* - that was big in his time. And you would ask me a few times, "well what ,, what's he *mean* by that?" .. "what's *that* all about?"

.. *um* you have a sense of what .. what he meant by that at all? ..

JB: - no ,, not really .. *!!*

CB: - Because .. I *did* find a passage - it was
Remarkable,
in the book.

He said, "No one's interested in *Suggestion.*
No one wants to know about *Suggestion . . ."*
and . . .

He's, it's really trying to <u>discount</u> it -
tremendously! and then he refers to these two
people who were big in the field of *Hypnosis* at
that time .. right when it was switching from
Mesmer (who believed it was the power of the
operator, some mystical power) when it
started switching over to a 'What-are-the-
Talents within-the-Person!'

Then he mentioned two Researchers, that I
have labeled in the earlier part of our writing,
here. People can check on that and see how
the field was ...was developing.

But I think Freud, though well-trained in that hypnosis-of-the-*day,* he was really discounting it *tremendously,* and that has *lasted.*

How many people are interested, especially Freudian analysts - though I do know, some - how many *know hypnosis*?

JB: I don't think they deal *at all* with hypnosis.

CB: Well I think you're right, except *uh* the U of Chicago people, my school, they, many knew *Erica Fromm* and they learned a *little bit* of hypnosis, through her. So there is an exception..
         ((*Check " **Erica Fromm** " in Wikipedia.))*

.. Chicago Psychoanalytic Institute, in some cases, but mostly *no,* they don't deal with it.

CB: .. and, do you still have a negative view of it?

JB: Pretty *much.*

CB: Because you.. do you remember where that *comes* from?

JB: Well I think I told you, that it was .. / *CB:* yes you did / .. when I studied psychology as an undergraduate, when I mentioned that to my professor, he warned me, he says oh don't touch it .. He said, it was "very, very dangerous," .. "*not* to touch it."

CB: ..and was he, was he a *Freudian* at all?

JB: I don't really *know*..

CB: Because that was .. that was *y'know* maybe a concern, back in the fifties (1950s). I think around 1955 *the A.M.A. accepted hypnosis* as a valid principle.

 ((SEE: **Hypnosis in Contemporary Medicine - Mayo Clinic** *))*

———————————

- *1955* – The **British Medical Association** became the **first professional organization**   to endorse the medical use of hypnosis.
- *1958* – The **American Medical Association** officially approved hypnosis as a therapeutic procedure (Along w/ other policies, may have been rescinded.)
- *1958* – The **Canadian Medical Association** endorses hypnosis.
- *1958* – The **Canadian Psychological Association** endorses hypnosis.
- *1960* – The **American Psychological Association** endorses hypnosis.
- *1961* – The **American Psychiatric Association** endorses hypnosis as a therapeutic procedure.

((SEE: Other Internet Resources for further History & details.))

But you're right, there were a lot of people very negative about it. I'm not so hep or hap with *authoritarian* hypnosis; I've never really been interested in that (form of it).

And my form of hypnosis, I used to say partly wistfully, was how to get *out* of hypnosis - But now it's not wistful it's very clear*!* -that there *is a way* to be *less* in hypnosis .. Of life and of culture .. by getting in touch with this more *free and clear place!*

So I don't really do hypnosis (per se); I do something Erica Fromm called, "*Hypnoanalysis*" & she started the idea on it.

It's a way of helping people more *quickly* get in touch with their *inner* realities - things that they like to find in the Freudian hypnosis, and she had a quicker way, called "*Permissive hypnosis.*"

And my (own) development was more, "..Well let's ask the *Question*," instead of waiting 10 years to see what comes up in some of the *ramblings* or some of the *great discussions* .. What about asking, "Well what does this *Mean?*"

And that was & is .. has been *my style.*

So I'm not negative about using - the process - in a in a *good* way; I'm not so positive on *authoritarian* hypnosis at all.

But do you think *that* got in through Freud?
Because he makes some *very* negative
comments about hypnosis which he is calling
"Suggestion."

 ((" *that* " = *the Highly Negative attitude
about Hypnosis*

 and its derivatives.))

JB: I think Freud is afraid .. that you might be
influencing the child. I think he wants to get ..
wants to find out what's going on in the child's
mind.

CB: Well I wish that were *true* but with little
Hans what I see, and I think *you were* seeing,
is that little Hans *is* getting influenced. ..
would be nice- he did say to the-

JB: Huh*!* yes*!* -that's why I- I think we agree,
that *this* is not a very good *argument* for,
psychoanalysis.

 ((*"this"* = *All about Little Hans from pg 1 to
100*))

CB: And one *positive* thing he said to the
parents, one or both - if you're offering your

child as kind of an experimental subject, I'd like you to raise him with the "minimal amount of coercion," 'cause he wanted to get a *natural*

..

JB: Yeah*!*

CB: So that was, as it turns out, a much more than modern way *any*way. But I don't know if -

JB: Sure*!*

CB: - I don't think he was that committed to it b'cause he was in a very authoritarian culture at the time.

It was kind of radical - "Raise him with minimum coercion."

JB: Hym-hymm*!*

CB: But the question was.. That there was a *lot* of *influence* there .. going on.

And *you'know* in discussing this with *you* over the past period of time .. I realized, there's something I learned in *1971 or '72*, it was so *obvious* to me at the time, but not I realize, maybe it's not so obvious. Maybe most people (in the field) don't realize this.

I was working with Pupil Services, as a clinician, and there was one kindergarten where *20 kids* were referred from *one teacher* to *pupil services for services!*

That would be very expensive, and People in pupil services were almost mortified - or very concerned - so they asked, well what if I would do some classroom observation? Which I did.

-does this ring a bell at all? / *JB:* no. / okay ..

CB: -so I went there, and what I was seeing was, the teacher was saying things, and the kids were *acting out* what this teacher *was saying.* I wish I'd remember all the details but like here's a case maybe *example,* where the teacher would use an idiom, saying you know like, "knock yourselves out," and then the kids would run around in circles and knock themselves out.

Whatever she said, they would take *very literally!*
/ *JB:* Hymm!/ .. and I started pointing it out to the teacher, and to pupil services, and I worked with her on that.

So to me it (became) very obvious / *JB:* hym-hymm!/ I didn't even know hypnosis at *that* time, and was just beginning to study family therapy.
   *((**Family therapy** for the first two years))*

But ever since it was like a *given* - that adults *are* going to *influence,* especially little kids. There is an influence there. The kids *do want to comply.* And it's important to be careful with what the words *are* that are being *sent.*

JB: I think in this case with little Hans, their comments by Freud and by the father - which are *very directive!* - and I think would be

something from my perspective, would not be
.. *not* be advisable*!*

CB: ... yeah*!* So that's ... I *totally agree* with
that.
(*17:06*)

… like they don't quite recognize it, or they're
so much into proving the theory … like when
Little Hans said to his father, "Is Freud .. does
he talk to God?!"
Lol - that's earlier I forget what page that's on

That came up because Freud said to little
Hans, "Before you were born, *I knew* that *you
would want* to .." paraphrasing, "marry your
mother, or be very close to your mother, and
get rid of your father."

Basically he was talking about his Oedipal
schmediple theory, and little Hans said - they
called him "The Professor" - *how*, how would
the Professor *know that,* know *what I think,*
basically, or know about that before I was even
born??

So Freud says, he could be flattered by that statement about this *"Does Freud talk to God?"* except that he was kind of tooting-his-own-horn maybe a little bit, and aware that maybe he was talking a little *too positive {* *laughing }* about himself ...

But I wouldn't be flattered by that; I would say "Hans is right on," *you'know.* - That's one of the *best examples* of what you're talking about: *i n f l u e n c i n g* Little Hans, over-influencing him.

JB: And the father does this also.

CB: Yeah .. yeah*!* - Because the father is an adherent of Freudian Theory.

And Freud only did it when he saw him that *one* time - once or twice - and then he made that comment that I just said. So the father does that throughout the whole so-called *analysis.. / JB: um-hymm. /*

CB: And as you asked, did the father ever analyze anybody else? I don't think so.

Yeah, so those things came up, and I don't think they realized *you-know,* **what** they were doing, in that .. The Influence on the little child ..

JB: **Right!**   / *CB:* So ..

CB: So The reader, or listener will hear more of the *details* of what we have covered in the first 100 pages ..

.. but we are about to, you and I, embark on Section III ..
Freud's Discussion. / *JB:* um-hymm. /

CB: .. and I'm looking at that with a little trepidation because Freud already acknowledges he's **not** going to share certain things that *won't* prove his theory. He's going to *simplify it* so he can make some certain statement.

But he's already proven to us in the first hundred pages that it *hasn't* proven his point. And now he's going to even use Little Hans *less* - or sometimes he refers to a prior page - and we've checked *all* those "prior pages" *out,* that he that he refers to; and we never find that it *is* proving his point*!*

CB: . . . So . . . (*lol, my laugh*) . . . *umm*

So I hope we've given, or I've given, and we've given, a little bit of an advance notice what we're *dealing* with ..

Because, I really have *enjoyed,* with you, going over the first *100* pages .. where Little Hans was *speaking up.*

We're not getting a *transcript,* exactly, like with most of my 20-some cases, but we are getting some good details on .. on this *one* case of *little Hans.* And it's been very enjoyable - - to hear from 'Little Hans.'

*JB: R*ight.

CB: And now we're going to hear from just 'big Sigmund' - - for the next *fifty* pages.

So therefore I asked you, could you on your own, do a review of what you see on page 118?

You don't like to leave messages but I reminded you, well this was your plan, and it *was* your plan, and you left the great 3-minute message on what you saw on face 118. And you said, why do you need why would you need me to say that on my own? and I was thinking the same thing of *influence.* I wanted to see *you-know,* what you said *without me* on the call, the things that *you view.*

And again, you were very consistent, and you also very very right on about the things you .. you observed about 10 different things on page 118.

.. and if they haven't heard that already that will come next, in transcript form or audio form.

So, does that make any sense to what I just said? *You-know* I wanted to get your *own* point on it. About what you thought of Little Hans and what you thought of Sigmund *in this situation* - only with Hans.

JB: Well I think we have to nail it down to something a little bit more particular.

CB: You mean the whole thing?

JB: Well I mean for me to respond, look at a sentence here or a concept, that he expresses here, and see what Freud's response is, I'll be glad to talk about *that*.

You-know I think we want to stick to detail here, not general impressions .. I think we *have g*iven the general impression here, namely that *ah,* there doesn't seem to be *evidence* of the Freudian theory in the responses of this child*!*

CB: Okay .. yeah, I'm *with you on that.*

B'cause I do want to get to .. we have covered *some* details, but I think we get to a lot *more* as we go. We have covered some *basic Impressions.*

But they'll be a *lot more* if people want to go into that great degree of detail .. *details.*

Because that's what Freud does*! He goes into so much detail that nobody probably has the* wherewithal *LOL, to deal with them, And at the time he was the guy who was expressing what the* inner world *was about* and what psychology was about.

So yeah we'll get into all of those, into most of those, details .. and .. I don't know if there's anything else, in terms of the *General* picture right now.

Oh!, just in Conclusion.

So .. so you still have a belief in Freud's theories *like* the *oedipal complex,* and you still think ..

JB: Yeah. Right.

CB: .. those are for *real,* and I did want to ask you, well where do you think you *got that* from*?*

JB: I think that was from when I studied *psychology,* as an undergraduate. I think it was *generally accepted* psychoanalytic theory.

CB: So it was generally accepted*!* ..

JB: Oh Yeah*!*

CB: .. as the *only* theory*!*
   - right?   /   *JB:* Well ..

JB: .. yeah, I would say it was the predominant theory.

CB: .. and what, are you talking about the 'fifties, or ..?

JB: Yeah .. right.

CB: ..because I did want to get back to one thing I had mentioned earlier about my *Neo-freudian.* Because I studied it in the late 60s, originally, '68 to '70 at U of Chicago.

They already were into *derivations.* I *didn't realize* that we were doing something *radically different.* But it was *not* the simple *you- know* conventional, hard-and-fast Freud - where you make the "unconscious conscious."

And that once you do that, everything works *out.* And then, you *follow the Authority!*

Am I wrong there?
 ..'cause we've had lots of talks on *that.*

JB: I don't know what you mean about, *"following the authority?"*

CB: .. not so much just the authority of Freud, *but ..* Once you get all the "unconscious conscious," then you *follow the authority of the society!*
You know, you fit *in* ..

JB: Oh, sure, yeah.

CB: .. And don't forget, I'm a child of the Sixties, And in the late 60s we were not quite as *concerned* about "fitting in." It was more of a *radical time* . and .

Whoever came up with the curriculum at U of Chicago was rather .. amazing .. when they brought in Eric Erickson to it to talk about the *Eight Stages of Man.*
   ((SEE: **"Eight Stages of Man"** - *via Wikipedia))*

He was "a Freudian." He studied with Anna Freud, but he talked about the *Eight stages.* And he tied in the Oral, Anal, Oedipal *to* Trust, Initiative .. He tied it into actual behavioral operations, and tied it in across the *whole life cycle.*

So that's when I first started learning about *my version* of Freud .. then you add in the Transactional Analysis .. So I never did get the

same training you did, that was more
"conventionally Freud."

-if I'm using the right word - "conventionally" -
or very close to an adherent of what Freud ..
how he put it originally.

And then, I don't know if you still believe about
"fitting in with" the culture .. And that was
Freud's .. aim..?

JB: Oh, s u r e.

CB: .. that was his *Aim* ..?

JB: Oh, a *b s o l u t e l y.*

CB: .. so .. uhh .. (*lol - laughingly*) so you say
that with a lot of ... *e n e r g y!*

JB: That was .. yeah*!* .. you lived in a
Society, and there were certain *standards,* and
you had to *adjust* your .. *you'know*, to
discipline yourself .. to fit into the standards of
the society.. unless..

- Unless they were things that were *y'know, immoral or uh,* some reason *not* to ..

But for the most part, you try to fit yourself into the pattern of society .. If you want to be part of the society then you had to adjust to its *pattern*.

CB: And that's what Freud's *aim* was, right?

JB: Yeah*!* I think, in part. ..

CB: Well how do you think *he* fit in .. *?*
And, what's your view *now* - when you look at people and how they fit in or don't fit in .. *?*
 ~
Do you think you've changed your views at all, on that*?*

JB: I don't think so.. No.

CB: .. Because we're talking about pre-Nazi time .. when his .. his theories were *there ..* *um. you know,* Hitler was just coming to power .. in his part of the world ..

And to fit into *that* society would be *immensely* pathological.

JB: .. oh Absolutely*!* ..

CB: So now .. *these* days .. we're not so much dealing with *repression { lol, laughter }* .. Everybody says whatever the hell they want to *say ..or do..* and *do wha.. y'know* do the whole *drug-thing and everything else.*

.. even in the *sixties* there were a lot of *drugs* ..
~

CB: So that's probably a whole 'nother discussion .For another time . but I think that is a good one . About "fitting into society" - - versus something *else!*

And if we do kind of, tear apart some of Freud based upon little Hans, if we don't, if you don't, find something better, Don't find better proof then - - I'm saying we have something else To offer, that comes from, partly Freud, comes from Heinz Kohut, and comes from me.

———

((I recently have begun looking into **Anna Freud** even the last few days, and her Concepts, including about the **SELF**.))

((**SSV** - the natural **Organic** Inner **SELF** - "The Still,Soft Voice."))

———

And that is . the self, S e l f.

*-which is somewhat separate; it knows how to deal with society . But it's **not** a complete reflection of society .*

-as let's say, the conscience. The super-ego is pretty much a reflection of the groups that one hangs around.

-Where the S e l f comes from a different place.

Heinz Kohut would have a lot have a lot to say about that, and I have a different take - that it's an organic part, Of the person.

………... But we'll get to all that………...
So anything else, before we conclude this, and get back to some details?

JB: .. no.

CB: .. ok .. *and uh ..*

JB: Clearly it doesn't work if you're living in an evil Society.
  CB: right.   *JB:* The assumption is that the society is *uh-you-know* a *sensible* one ..

CB: ..well ..as I'm looking at it out there, it doesn't seem.. It seems less and less sensible .. *um .. you-know like* right now there's a .. almost an emotional Civil War .. between the different parties, and they stop communicating With each other, the Right and the Left.

.. for instance, and it's almost a *Shutdown* of communication ..

JB: I agree - - that's a very *bad* and *dangerous* circumstance.

CB: So if someone fits in to either one-half or the other- half Of society, I also agree, it *is* both bad and dangerous.

If somehow they can relate to *both* aspects, I think you and I would probably agree, that's a *Healthier* place to be ~ !

JB: Well somewhere in-between.

CB: yeah and . . . I'm a . . . I'm an an Old-style liberal, kind of like yourself, I believe they should be *talking* with each other and coming up with …

JB: Absolutely*!*

CB: … S*olutions* that they both can *agree* on
…

JB: Absolutely*! 100* percent*!*

CB: … *you-know* … and *stick with* what they each think … and then come to something they each can tolerate*!*

JB: Absolutely.

CB: …It's *much healthier.*
          ..so..   *JB:* ..agreed.

Again that's a little more *dynamics;* one can work Freud into that in terms of *wish* and *fear,* one group taking the *wish* and one group taking the *fear.*

But that's beyond *our* paper, our work right now ..
So *thanks a lot* for sharing some more *Basics* here*!*

JB: Okay*!*

CB: And then we'll get back to some of the *details.*

As they say or I say, *God is in the details.*

JB: agreed.   *CB:* okay!   *lol*

I hope we .. this recording
        will *hold* for us; thanks a lot.   *JB:*
right.

PREFACE

Baby Hans
C h r o n o l o g y
- SF's page 4 of 150 -

1903	(April) Hans born.
1906	(Age 3 - 3¾) First Reports.
	(Age 3¼ - 3½) (Summer)
	1st visit to Gmunden.
	(Age 3½) Castration threat.
	(Age 3½) (October) Hanna born.
1907	(Age 3¾) First dream.
	(Age 4) Removal to new flat.
	(Age 4¼ - 4½) (Summer)
	2nd visit to Gmunden.
	Episode of biting horse.
1908	(Age 4¾) (January)
	Episode of falling horse.
	'Outbreak of phobia.'
	(Age 5) (May) End of analysis.

~

Freud's Fallacy

God is in the details

A deeper look at the actual baby Hans

Okay we're starting and we're recording..
We talked about really getting into the details.

CB: -as I say, *"God is in the details."*
.. of Little Hans *in conjunction with* or vis-à-vis ..
Sigmund Freud. We can now take a look at *some*
of the issues and some of the theories, as it
applies specifically to the *d a t a* of little Hans.

Now, there is something else.

When he gets to Part 3 he's speaking *only* about
his own views and his own theories. And as you
(JB) just pointed out, in a very Basic introduction,
there too he's introducing it *only from his point of
view.*

So I think we should get to that .. maybe next,
and that will be Freud only himself speaking. I

think there is a kind of a risk *scientifically* in that because then you're only getting it from the person who some call "The Professor" or the "Master" or the "Father" of psychology or psychiatry.

And then people tend to be influenced by that. But we can cover that too .. next.

So right now, I guess we're both ready to really look at some of the details of some of the theories … as applies to little Hans or as little Hans *reacts* .. or the *Data*…given.

CB: .. so ..ready?   *JB:* Ready   *CB:* okay (*little laugh*) So ..
The first of a few issues would be about … penis … basically.

PENIS - (Widdler?)

Some people get upset when we talk about "penis so much," even though that's very much a part of Freud's vocabulary and approach. In one of the reading groups there was a very nice young lady, who said *you-know* ".. I dropped out of the reading group because there was so-much-*penis* in it.."

(mutual laughter)

- and.. nice lady too!

JB: Should have said *"widdler!"* (*lol*)
CB: (*laughing*) Yeah .. maybe .. try to use the
English word ..

And then I we laughed and she pointed to the picture
of Freud over our shoulder .. and the facilitator and
we're all saying, "Well that's a big part of *Freud* .."

JB: and he asks (*page 7*),
"Mummy, have you got a widdler too?"

And she says, *"Of course .."*
  [".. Why do you ask?"]

JB: now if he's referring to the *penis,* why should she
say that she *"has."* =?=

CB: So we're on page 7 .. and that was one of the
first things *we* came up with.

JB: ohh .. is that right.   *CB: you* and *me.* Some
time ago ..

*CB: ..*and I think we were looking at the *German* for
"widdler" - and I'll talk later about the Brickman
household & the use of the word "wig*gler,*" years and
years ago, which is more accurate I think -

But do you remember what you noticed in footnote 1 there at the bottom?

JB: no

CB: it says *"'Wiwimacher' in the original."*

JB: Oh! ... So *that's* what he asked her .. hah*?!*

CB: So you pointed out, "Hymm I think the *(..diagnosis LOL not diagnosis, but the)* *translation* of that would be: *"wee-wee-macher,"* the
> *' Wee-wee maker '*

JB: Yeah. So *that's* what she says she has - hah*!*

CB: So you're the one .. well I noticed the..the German .. and you're the one who came up with that *translation*, which makes perfect sense
> *' Wee-wee maker '*

JB: Hym-hymm.

CB: So all through this (English) translation, we're reading *"widdler,"* and
how often in the German was it actually *'Wee-wee maker'* that Hans was asking about? and that the mommy was responding to.

JB: -emm!

CB: Because originally I was thinking, many of us were thinking, the mother was *lying* and saying she had a penis - when she didn't - and how confusing that would be to the young boy.

Very confusing, and that's a big part of Freud's theories of .. homosexuality excetera excetera .. and here we look at this little footnote page 7
Wee-wee maker..!!

So … That makes more sense*!*   *JB:* *-Yeah!*

CB: By definition - - "That which makes *wee-wee*." *(*
mutual laughter)
        JB: -Yeah.   *CB:* - as compared to
"Widdler."

Now in my family our family, growing up, I think you used the word *Wiggler.* And it was - *we all kind of laughed* - and at least *that's more accurate.*
   JB: -True!   *CB:* ..because, it *wiggles ..!*   *(laugh)*

That's more like... That's a penis, in a young baby, a young boy, a man   hatever, some of the time.

.. and *uh* .. where "widdler" to me is *completely* other than representing or sounding like wiggler, it.. How does that *Enlighten* anything?

.. *you-know* why would they use that as a *translation?*
-

JB: I have no idea.

CB: -unless they feel that the Americans at that time were so uptight, they couldn't use the word *"penis" lol* themselves .. or, *"Wee-wee maker."*

So then you and I started talking, some time ago, about "What's the difference between *urethra* and the *penis?"* ..or even with the female..

We *are* getting into details here now, folks - *Medical details* - "What's the difference between the .. *clitoris* and the *urethra?"* Those are *two separate* organs!

I hope that Freud realized that.

JB: I'm sure he ..realized it.

CB: Well I don't *know* .. *You-know* he went through *hundreds of eels* when he when he was in .. I think it was botany or some other science, before he got into this [it was **Zoology**].

And his instructor wanted to see if he could *find* in the *eel* .. where, where the male and female sexual organ was. Now maybe he didn't tell him or maybe did -

- For hundreds of years they were looking for that and could never find it. It was only recently they realized it was in a *[morphological]* structure that was hard to find. So I hope he realizes, realized that 'cuz I think Freud made a parallel between the *clitoris* and the *penis.*

And that was before he *did realize* because nobody knew that the Clitoris is not that *tiny little thing* that might change a *little* bit .. but it's connected to a whole Labyrinth of clitoral Connection in the background .. or underneath it all.

So I don't think he knew *that!*

So this was a big *thing* - the whole idea of "Penis" - "the Wee-wee maker" - and so we see on page 7 here.

Hans is saying, *"Mummy have you got a widdler too?"*

And mother says, *"Of course. Why?"*
Hans says, *"I was only just thinking.."*

And then the next paragraph says, at the same age he went into a cowshed once and saw a cow being milked, *"Oh look,"* he said, *"there's milk coming out of its widdler."*

Now in that case there might be more of a visual parallel there, with the male organ.

JB: He's got the two of them confused obviously.

CB: Well yeah, and I don't think anyone helps clarify that.

Actually the mother the father and Freud agreed at some point, that they're *not* telling him the details. And much *later* Freud suggested, 'well, give him the details.

Because meanwhile, he's getting very confused - he's a very *smart* little boy - as we both were realizing - and you give him a little piece of wrong information he'll *go with it* - try to figure it out. Later it's about a *Stork!*

Umm so he's trying to figure it out - and then - now he's labeled with some of the other Freudian concepts related to this: Penis obsession, fear of cas.. Castration anxiety, and all these things that when you and I were going through this I don't think either one of us really ..saw that.

Does that ring a bell to you, does that seem right?

JB: I don't remember about the castration.

CB: Because it was about a lot of different things. so maybe we can go over this again, not exactly re-create it but *create it* and show the listener, the reader, exactly how we're looking at things.

Because the first hundred pages, we looked at it a number times for me, and for both of us, in *great depth*.

Y o u r Qu e s t i o n s

And any question that somebody has - whether in the field, whether Freudian, whether a casual reader, or whether this is the first time, we're *happy to respond* to, right?

JB: - Right*!*

CB: We talked about .. even on the *Amazon site* -
for people not just to leave a Review of our work - but
to leave *any Questions* .. any *Comments* that they
want to have further discussed.

And I think that's a good way to get further
communication on this, from both the professional
realms as well as the public in general.

JB: Um-hymm. -

CB: So we are inviting people to Interact with us - -
and then we'll also keep revising the book from time
to time, as well.

~

So that's a little bit on The Wiggler.

Do we want to continue with this .. or go on to
another, to the next Topic what do you think?   / *JB:*
.. you decide ..

Okay we were just discussing .. I think we should
probably cover a little more on wigglers, or as they
say here, Widdlers, since it is so basic to Freud.

There are a couple of things of interest as Freud puts out.

So the bottom of page 7,
"Meanwhile his interest in widdlers was by no means a purely theoretical one. It also impelled him to touch *his member .."*

So you have any thoughts on that?   *JB:* no.

CB: Because ..they were, they weren't encouraging him, "..Don't touch yourself. It's not something to do, in public." And at that time they were pretty ..late 1800s early 1900s, they were pretty *strict* about such things. So they're trying to get him not to touch..his penis.

Now Freud is saying, he was *impelled* to touch his member - because of his *interest* -   *JB:* hm-hymm..

- where you and I originally were talking about, "well it *feels* good." So that's another reason or maybe the *main* reason..   *JB:* hm-hymm.   / ..why he felt like touching, his penis.   *JB:* Right.

"So when he was three-and-a-half .."
- do you want to do this at the bottom or should I ..
JB: go ahead.

CB: So .. *"When he was three-and-a-half, his mother found him with his hand on his penis."* -they are using the word penis there, they didn't say widdler- *"She threatened him in these words: "*

- and to me this is *very Important* as a family therapist, as someone who deals with *trauma* and interaction of- *JB:* yeah! -parent and child.

"If you do that, I shall send. for Dr. A. to cut off your widdler. And then what'll you widdle with?"

JB: That's a *terrible* thing to say to a kid*!*

CB: Yeah*!* ..and yet It seems to go by.. when people read this, they don't realize how terrible that is*!* - - That's pretty..pretty messed up *!!*

JB: Yeah, to cut off .. cause a kid to have a *castration complex!*.

CB: Yeah*!* and *that's* where the *Castration complex* could come from .. Not from his..his *Inner* world; came from his *Outer* world.

JB: Right.

CB: So .. and that's.. *you-know*… I.. look *first* at that sort of thing .. *you-know*…Traumatic ..*Cause.* And I think Freud may be .. maybe *used* to look at that, and then started *minimizing* it-

JB: -It's interesting- , he doesn't discuss it at all ..

CB: Yeah that's *very* interesting ..
- that it's kind of just .. *overlooked..!*

JB: yeah.

CB: When I first read this I brought it up in the reading discussion group there at the Analytic Institute, I said, "W o w*!* to me, a Parent says something like that *one time* .. is enough for a permanent..*trauma* and a permanent.."

JB: -a -What did the class *uh* think?   *CB:* "..and a permanent..*Imprint.*"

CB: Well I think the people didn't *uh* didn't quite go along with my.. But of course there aren't many other therapists there - and there's no other Family therapist - and no *trauma specialist* - So I don't really ..doesn't matter *lol* .. to me *too* much ..what they think. ..but I think they were going by the group .. and .. *you know* the professor or the person from the Psy.. -shall I use his name-

Dr Galatzer-Levy. I like a lot of what he says .. but I don't think he took it *quite* as *seriously* as *I took it.* So I.. I made it very clear that,
>   *That's* a major.. *Major Issue!*

JB: - *Y e a h !* - for sure *!!*

CB: So then Hans says .. *(.. continuing, page 8) ..*
     [-the Mother -according to the Father -according to S. Freud]:
     "*.. What will you widdle with?*"

Instead of - are you now traumatized.. ?,
Hans says, "With my bottom."

JB: - So in effect he'd be a *female* -

CB: Well I don't know..if he took it that far .. *Maybe..-*
-
That's interesting .. or is he thinking of the Wee-wee maker .. that the wee-wee maker comes out of the *bottom.* But that's a *good point.* I mean that's really very..very anatomically *smart lol* if he meant that.

CB: *(.. continuing on page 8) ..*
.. and then Freud's comment was,
"He made this reply without having any sense of guilt, as yet. But this was the occasion his acquiring the

*'castration complex', the presence of which we are so often obliged to infer in analyzing neurotics [add: "though they one and all **struggle violently against it"**]."*

But..I don't think Freud is acknowledging .. that he *acquired* this through his *Mother's **statement**.!*

He's thinking he acquired it through his response to the mother.. in.. in (via) *Han's statement!*

But this could be discussed in great detail, from different points of view. But that's in the next number of paragraphs and so on.

.. and then Freud is saying *[paraphrasing], 'Well I thought this all along because this is what I was proclaiming in the Interpretation of Dreams ..'* excetera.

- And then you can go into these footnotes etc - *which we did* - but I don't want to lose the reader by being so much in the weeds …as important as these *Weeds, are …*

So if anyone wants to discuss that further, we could. And then they talk about Hans going to the *zoo.*

JB: Let's finish this paragraph first.

CB: Okay ... go ahead ..

JB: S. Freud,
"There is much of importance to be said upon the significance of this element in the life of a child. The 'castration complex' has left marked traces behind it in myths (and not only in the Greek myths); in a passage in my Interpretation of Dreams [1900] ... "

CB: "*... and elsewhere, I have touched upon ....*"

JB: - Yeah maybe we should look into *that*.
   CB: "*.... the part it plays.*"

CB: - Well we actually *did* look into *everything* that he brings up, and then we get back to ..

JB: "I have touched upon the part it plays."   *CB:* well ..
     JB: - Want to talk about that footnote there number 3?

CB: Yeah... *okay* maybe that will give people *uh* an example, we do go back & look at stuff and then ..
JB: I have Question marks here ..
     CB: .. and then we decide *you-know,* does it prove what he's saying? 'Cause he's referring back to .. him*self* .. his *own* theory.

But yeah .. go ahead ..

JB: *[Footnote 2 - bottom half of page 8]*
"Since this was written, the study of the castration complex has been further developed in contributions to the subject by Lou Andreas-Salomé [1916], A. Stärcke [1910], F. Alexander [1922] and others.

CB: -and this footnote was added in 1923- *you-know* 15 years *after* the study of 'Little Hans,' so you and I can keep talking about that but I'll put this on hold, so we don't get so far into the weeds again that people will not be interested. So should we continue this or - ?-

JB: Sure.

CB: Okay.. I guess I can keep recording, and then just remove it.
So go ahead, yeah ..   *[kept everything]*

JB: " ..It has been urged that every time his mother's breast is withdrawn from a baby he is bound to feel it as castration .."*

-   *JB:* -and that's what, I have a Question mark there - Where do you .. what's the connection? Why would he *uh* he feel that a mother's breast is withdrawn -the baby can no longer suckle-

why would he feel that is <u>*castration*</u>*?* I don't understand that at all*!*

CB: Well this is like *theory* upon *theory* upon *theory*, and I don't even think this is Freud's theory; this is by a proponent of Freud.

-but I *agree* with you. It doesn't prove *anything;* it just adds a little bit of *uh* .. -what's the word .. -texture? - Confusion? *uh* -an extra image .. ?
-okay so, you want to continue on that ..

JB: -on the footnote here?
CB: -if you want to, yeah ..

CB: - 'Cause again, I don't think this proves the point- Because the original point, that gets *lost* in this kind of writing- is, the mother says,

"*We're going to send you to Dr. A., he's going to cut off your penis, your widdler, and then you'll see what you widdle with.*"
     -and Hans says, "*With my bottom.*"

But Instead, they get into *all* of this very *elaborate* "*theortizing*" (theorizing), and they *never mention* about -again- what **Mom said** to her **little b a b y**.

JB: -hymm-

CB: And so it gets *lost* -literally- in the *(small lol)* translation, and in a 100 years of discussion - - how many people get back to the *basics? As* just mentioned.

And then this goes on for a while, in terms of *horses with widdlers, and dogs with widdlers,* and *noticing widdlers* and *uh ..*

JB: -and where are you?-
CB: .. *well* this is *that* page, the *next* page .. I'm just trying to ..
JB: .. *oh* the *next* page, not this footnote..?
CB: .. well you want to continue..? with the footnote ..
JB: -well except the footnote seems so sil- to be - gets off the subject, as it consists here, *wrong.*

CB: Yeah that's what *I'm* thinking ..also.
And, as we know, *you are* a *proponent* of Sigmund Freud, right?
JB: Right.
CB: and I'm *you-know,* I see him as a *Pioneer,* but I see some *problems ..* and my training was a little bit different, as we alluded to..

JB: -I wonder who *added* this thing in 1923, doesn't say that *he* added it. *CB:* right.

JB: It might have been done by somebody entirely different.

CB: Well it could have been by Sigmund, I guess; it could have been by Anna Freud; or it could have been by -who's the other main translator- would be Freud's friend.. *uh* …

~

CB: .. where is the Names of the translators .. *yeah* I thought there was a *Jones* who was involved in the translation ..but it says, "Under the general editorship of **James Strachey**, in collaboration *with **Anna Freud**.*" -to me that's an important one- and then assisted by a couple of others, and an editorial assistant.

So, yeah! Who comes up with the translations? .. And who added this- who *added* this?   *JB:* Yeah. *CB:* And that's a long footnote! -which, we went through the whole thing, but-

JB: Yeah It's important to find out from *uh* ,, wonder if he has some earlier editions of the book, If they tell you, who wrote this.

CB: [*bit away from microphone*] Well they even get into the issue of *uh*.. should I read this? This, it might be useful; it is in that same footnote, ½ way into it.

JB: Yeah -go ahead-

CB: *"While recognizing all these roots of the complex, I have nevertheless[1] put forward the view that the term 'castration complex' ought to be confined to those excitations and consequences which are bound up with the **loss of the penis**."*
[-Sigmund Freud speaking, apparently-]

CB: .. *well*, kind of makes sense.   *JB:* yeah. *lol* ..   *CB:* ..on the surface.

[continuing],
*"Anyone who, in analyzing adults, has become convinced[2] of the invariable presence of the castration complex,will **of course find difficulty** in ascribing its **origin** to a chance threat -- of a kind which is not, after all, of such universal occurrence; he will be **driven to assume** that children construct this danger for themselves out of the slightest hints, which will never be wanting."*
[*Who ~ How ~* & *Why* were those who were *"convinced,"* convinced?]

CB: [*back to microphone*] So, so that whoever wrote that, is saying: well they **are** acknowledging the **threat** -in tiny little print- the ***"chance threat"*** from the mother*!* - they're *not* dealing with it *directly;* they're

---

[1] -S. Freud speaking, apparently-
[2] *How* & *why* were those convinced, convinced?

acknowledging it, *but* they're saying *w-e-l-l the* .. the little baby .. *uh* ..

JB: .. *that he*'ll hear it from *someone huh*? ..   *CB:* ..*that, what* .. ?
JB: -That he'll hear it from *some*one.

CB: -*t*hat,,well they're trying to say, "*-comes out of his own consciousness-*" I think, a deep consciousness hidden away in there *you know,* the Freudian *idea.*

However, if a *Freudian* person is *analyzing* the baby, it's more *likely* -or the adult- it's more likely to be *assumed!*

I think I mentioned to you, I did find something in a governmental site on Medicine and health, about taking a look at "Little Hans and Freud," (We don't, I don't, like to get *too much* into that because I want to have our *own, fresh* look, but-)

They did make a *General* statement, and maybe I can connect to it, here by clicking on it.. -that-

Future Freudians, I think it was Karen Horney? and others, *re*-evaluated *"Little Hans"* and they concluded, depending on the *theory* Of the person who's looking at it, *that's* what they come *up* with*!!*

JB: **-Laughter.**   *CB:* **-lol**

CB: -and it's done in a very cov-   *JB:* -Not very *scientific* hah?

CB: -Well- they *say* it very scientifically.
- will try to send that to you too.

~

So what *we're* trying to do is **not use a theory** - other than like family .. *family* therapy or *reality* therapy - just looks at- *uh,* what's the ..

JB: -the **evidence.**

CB: - the **evidence** and what's the *trauma*?
I mean, it's more *"superficial."*

Post-traumatic Stress Disorder looks at,
    -   What was the original *cause* of it .. ?

Now that doesn't mean there can't be some other stuff connected to it -childhood stuff and things like that- you've got to work with- But what's the **simple c-a-u-s-e**. And that's the one to deal with the *most!*

We've found that in Combat vets, *uh* Auto accidents, Rape victims, *you-know,* **how** to deal with that. We've spent like-a *year* on dealing with this, sometimes one piece of it. I could see spending *months* on this issue, like when Mom says,

> *"We're going to send you to Dr. A. to cut your widdler off ."*

We don't want to *push* that idea [as an example] but slowly-by-slowly at the rate that the patient *wants* to deal with it, to get it out of their system, emotionally as well as intellectually; that's how we often *deal* with Post-Traumatic Stress Disorder.

And that's what they left *out!* They're not really *dealing* with this*!*

JB: .. *yeah!!* - It's a **biggie.**

CB: *Yeah,* And you and I *agree on this,* even though we have, slightly different approaches to Freud - as a major Foundation of our work.

So I'm sure we'll have a lot more to say as we go *uh* at the end of this book as well as in the future, about some spiritual and theoretical ideas - about what was *left out* and what was *focused on,*

So I do think the negative was focused on but *this* was pretty negative - an important negative - the threat to cut off his *penis*, his widdler.

~

So .. maybe it's good we got into some of the *Detail*.
That's what we did, we got into *all* the details[3] ..
[Pages 1 to 100 so far.]

And every time we do, this is kind of what we find.

It's very tempting to get into more and more of this
part. But we're already about 30 minutes into this; that's a *lot*.
Because I was thinking we could fit *all* of these Concepts into
30 minutes which is about maybe 20 or 30 pages. I guess
there's no way to do that.

So at least we covered the *"Castration anxiety."* We
covered the issue of where things *come from.*

I *would* like to get, either *now* or in the future (let's
see, it's now, almost 5:00) into a **Prime thing** - - which
is the *Oedipal*-schmoedipal *Complex.*
Uh shall we do that *now-*

JB: Sure!   *CB:* -a little bit *?*

CB: We could find that in the book somewhere, and
there's even a nice picture of *(lol)* a horse that looks
like to me, a giraffe with a picture that was drawn ..
that's on page 13 .. of the "widdler" and *why* that
relates to "father" -supposedly- and then *[turning*

---

[3] Pages 1 to 100 so far.

pages] there's down the road also another picture of the **Bridle** of the horse that Freud thinks is related to the father's **mustache ...** and things like this.

JB: Yeah, I thought that part was a little bit, **contrived!**

CB: Yeah, yeah. We both thought that.
Pretty **contrived** - - when we can start with *simpler..*ideas.

So. I believe this *"Castration complex"* as it, certainly as it relates to the *Oedipal:* the assumption is, the father wants to cut off the penis because the baby *boy* especially, wants to kill the *father.*

Now what you think *(lol)* about *that* theory?
JB: Well they don't have it *here.*

CB: yeah *I mean* that's one of the theories but it's not proven *here,* with Little Hans, right?

JB: well it's not even *introduced!*
CB: well I think we could probably find it somewhere; I'll look it up in the index maybe for next time

But I did find something the other night, I sent you a video on it, that somebody talked about Freud and *Jung,* and what happened in *their* relationship - and *I believe* what happens in *any relationship* that kind of **believes this** or has this in the back of their mind -

- What father?, What son? -who believes this- could really relate freely openly lovingly and caringly, if they really think someone wants to cut their pecker off =or= wants to kill them.   :-)   { *laughing* }

Now you may not take it the same way, I don't know; do you think is more value in it?

JB: ... value in what?
CB: - in the *theory ?*

    . . .
- of the Oedipal, and the Castration -?-

JB: umm .. well I think there is some, *you-know* there is a *Rivalry* I think for the affection of .. of the kid and the father .. for the *mother's* affection

CB: Well I wouldn't, I wouldn't ..
JB: That's *genuine.*

CB: I think it can be made *worse* or be made *better.* You-know I think there's **competition *all over the place!***

-you know, with the **siblings** and even **between** *the* Mother and *the Father* of course, and the father and

the *son,* and the father and the ***daughter*** .. There's so much ***schtuff*** going on ..

But this *particular* Rivalry is made- is really <u>highlighted</u> and <u>exaggerated</u> -***magnified*** at least- by this *theory!*

~And, what happened with *Freud* and *Jung?*

The video I sent you, kind of answered a question that I had for some time. And that is, the time when Freud and Jung were meeting towards the end of their relationship. And Jung was making a point about Spiritual energy *Beyond* the obvious. And he said that, a bookcase would be cracking or breaking …?

JB: Oh yeah*! I remember that!!*

CB: And so, it did*!* ***Boom!*** And Freud was kind of *shocked.* And then he said, "Well-" and he didn't believe it. *"Coincidence!"*

.. so Jung said, *"If that's a coincidence, I think it's going to happen again!"* ***Boom!*** *It cracked again.*

And I believe Freud *fainted* at that time, at least that's what it said in the video. And he (Freud) thought that Jung wanted to *kill* him.
I don't know if that rings a bell at all ..

JB: No.

CB: ..but you do remember about the Bookcase.
JB: Yeah..

CB: I always wondered, why would he think that Freud, I mean Jung, wanted to kill him?
JB: I don't *k n o w !*

CB: .. and then on this video it says a little more, which kind of makes sense .. That Jung, at one point, says to Freud, "I want to be like your **son**. I'll treat you like my **father** rather than just as .. peers or.. colleagues*!"*

CB: .. I don't know if you remember *that part* of it.
JB: No, but he was his disciple so that was not far-fetched.. that way.

 CB: .. Yeah*!* Then I started thinking, *What does that mean?* in terms of Freud's theory.

That means that, the son wants to .. kill off .. the father.

And I think that was part of the *genesis* of their complete *break-off*. When Sigmund wrote Carl,

"I don't think we should talk anymore or relate any more.." and bye-bye.

It was the ancient version of what they do now, called *"Ghosting."*
-*lol,* the kids, and others-   So again, that- oh. How did that affect *them?*
- that *Oedipal assumption!*

~

-Though "Rivalry,"

I can go along with *Rivalry* and *issues*. But with a deeper look at things, such as *you know,* the *Yetzer Tov,*[4] not just the *Yetzer Hara,* as we've discussed, that *rivalry* can really turn into a much more of a positive kind of (thing) .. *Little* **competitive!** ~.

((*Yetzer Ha-Tov* and *Yetzer Ha-Ra*))   *I.e.,*
'The good inclination and the evil inclination' in the typical Rabbinic doctrine, with far-reaching consequences in Jewish religious thought ...'

---

[4] *Yetzer Ha-Tov and Yetzer Ha-Ra*
'The good inclination and the evil inclination.' In the typical Rabbinic doctrine, with far-reaching consequences in Jewish religious thought...

~ But that doesn't mean you-know ,, **destroying** the other person by any means*!* On the contrary.

So I don't know, do you have any, any other thoughts on that right now..
JB: no.
~

CB: So. I know this brings up a lot,, a lot, a lot of issues with the Freudian Theory, but I do like to get back to .. *Little Hans,* as you do.

And *uh* what should we cover next? maybe in our *Next* chapter - any thoughts on *What .. ?* Because we *have* covered *a lot* even in those first few pages and before the next 98 that we covered*!*
~

Yeah both of us were saying, *"It's pretty thin."* *You-know*, that wasn't much proof of *any* of these things - *not with Little Hans!*

And Little Hans did seem more *spiritual* when he talked about God, and he talked about, he said, *"What is the Professor's relationship with God?"* and excetera excetera

So.

Well that's a little more about *"God is in the Details."*
- and I'm not sure where to go from here - what page to look
at.
So should I put this on hold for now.

JB: **S~u~r~e.**

CB: And then we can look for more ..
        I'll put this on *"Hold."*

~

JB on page 118

- July 31 2019 Voicemail, 3 minutes
- 1st-ever by CB's Request

" *Hi Cliff , looking at this page one hundred eighteen..*
I just don't see where he sees *illness* in the youngster."

His being in bed with the mother, I think he just likes the *comfort* of her presence.. and *uh* I don't see where it's a *sexual thing at all* .. except (as) with other kids *y'know* like the *warmth* and the *presence* of the mother.

That's about all I can make of it. I don't see *where* he sees this as *traumatic* .. the fact that mother has gone away *[in a dream]*, and he *misses* her .. *?!* Seems to be quite normal.

"*..no-one [no mother] to coax with..*"
JB: I think that just means to *cuddle* with; I don't think it has to do with a *sexual* matter.

("the presence of") *"a repressive process of ominous intensity."* *("We cannot explain it..)*
JB: I don't know where that comes from.

" .. anxiety arising from some somatic cause .."
JB: I don't see where he feels anxiety.

"..from an unconscious wish.."
JB: I think his wish is quite *constant ..uh..*quite *conscious*!
.. mainly he likes having his mother with him. He likes her presence, her warmth, comfortings .. so .. I don't know what else I can say about that.

JB: I don't see where anything is pathological in this thing, at all. I don't see we have to look for anything *unconscious*. I think it's quite *conscious*.

JB: He just wants .. (*"he dreamt of"*) *"exchanging endearments with his mother.."* Of course, *"sleeping with her.. "* He just missed her when she was *away*.

"Repression had .."
JB: I don't see where there's any repression here.

("during the") "..previous summer.." ("psychological situation")
JB: .. Similar thoughts, but once again, I don't see where there's anything pathologic.

("We may assume that since then Hans had been in a state of ..") "..intensified <u>sexual excitement</u> .. the object of which was his <u>mother</u>."

JB: I don't think that's true at all.
I think he just missed her presence, child is comforted by that. I don't see anything here to assume that there's Illness .. psychological illness.. "

~

CB Addendum: S.F. says "We can easily reconstruct what actually occurred in the unconscious." [Of little Baby Hans in his dream]

CB: Not so fast. ~ And not so easy if at all.

POSTSCRIPT (1922)
[page 148 - 49]

Sigmund Freud:

A FEW months ago -- in the spring of 1922 -- a young man introduced himself to me and informed me that he was the 'little Hans' whose infantile neurosis had been the subject of the paper which I published in 1909. I was very glad to see him again, for about two years after the end of his analysis I had lost sight of him and had heard nothing of him for more than ten years. The publication of this first analysis of a child had caused a great stir and even greater indignation, and a most evil future had been foretold for the poor little boy, because he had been 'robbed of his innocence' at such a tender age and had been made the victim of a psycho-analysis.

But none of these apprehensions had come true. Little Hans was now a strapping youth of nineteen. He declared that he was perfectly well, and suffered from no troubles or inhibitions. Not only had he come through his puberty with-out any damage, but his emotional life had successfully undergone one of the severest of ordeals. His parents had been divorced and each of them had married again. In consequence of this he lived by himself; but he was on good terms with both of his parents, and only regretted that as a result of the breaking-up of the family he had been separated from the younger sister he was so fond of.

One piece of information given me by little Hans struck me as particularly remarkable; nor do I venture to give any explanation of it. When he read his case history, he told me, the whole of it came to him as something unknown; he did not recognize himself; he could remember nothing; and it was only when he came upon the journey to Gmunden that there dawned on him a kind of glimmering recollection that it might have been himself that it happened to. So the analysis had not preserved the events from amnesia, but had been overtaken by amnesia itself. Anyone who is familiar with psycho-analysis may occasionally experience something similar in sleep. He will be woken up by a dream, and will decide to analyze it then and there; he will then go to sleep again feeling quite satisfied with the result of his efforts; and next morning dream and analysis will alike be forgotten.

[This phenomenon was discussed by Freud in a passage added in 1911 to his *Interpretation of Dreams,* 1900a (Chapter VII, Section A; *Standard Ed., 5, 520-1).*]

OUR POSTSCRIPT (2019)
(*Of the Same pages 148-49*)

CB: Okay we're on *Record* and we're ready to go about taking a look at "Postscript 1922," and our comments will be "Postscript 2019."

JB: post-Postscript*!* :-)

CB: Yeah*!* Right*!* more recent Postscript. :-)

CB: So, so this is on page 148-49 ~ the final page-and-a-quarter of "Little Hans," who we call "baby Hans" ~ in the first half of the volume 10. Sigmund Freud's psychological works.

So here we are; we see *three* paragraphs; and as we've kind of discussed once before, the third paragraph is *uh* .. well we'll get to that .. *you-know* is it really having as much *gravitas* as the first *two* paragraphs?

But we'll get to that. I was thinking of having the Reader or the Listener listen to the whole thing … And seeing how it impresses them.

And then looking at it again, with our assistance, when we're analyzing what is being said*!* Because at first blush it all kind of hangs together until you really look at the *details.*

So, what I think *we're* doing, is we want to look at one paragraph at a time, and then, we'll go over all the details, in that paragraph.

JB: Okay ..

CB: So should .. do you want to read the 1st paragraph, and I'll read the 2nd .. or the other way around .. ?

JB: Sure. I'll read.

"A FEW months ago -- in the spring of 1922 -- a young man introduced himself to me and informed me that he was the 'little Hans' whose infantile neurosis had been the subject of the paper which I published in 1909. -

JB: .. This was written in 1922.

- I was very glad to see him again, for about two years after the end of his analysis I had lost sight of him and had heard nothing of him for more than ten years. The publication of this first analysis of a child had caused a great stir and even greater indignation, and a most evil future had been foretold for the poor little boy, because he had been 'robbed of his innocence' at such a tender age and had been made the victim of a psycho-analysis."

CB: So shall we analyze this 1st paragraph and then come back to the 2nd paragraph.

JB: Okay. I don't know anything *special* to say, about it.

CB: Ok, well I wrote some notes down when we spoke about it.

JB: Alright.

CB: -because I wasn't able to tape it at the time; this was a few days back, Sept 18.

CB: -So the first thing, that actually *you* pointed out was *"infantile neurosis!"* and I have that

in..in a box, in blue, *infantile neurosis* and I think *your* question, as is *mine*: **what** infantile neurosis?
(*laughing*)

JB: Right.*!* .. Right*!*

CB: -So you see when you read the whole thing *together* - and sometimes it's hard to take a look at these details. - But now that we-

JB: Umhym.

CB: -went over sentence by sentence .. you and I do see it very very much the same if not nearly 100% the same. So I thought .. I think you brought .. I had that in a box, and then you brought it up too*!*

"Infantile neurosis?" What does that mean; there's an assumption there-

JB: *R i g h t.*

CB: -that we haven't found to be *accurate*. It's an interesting *label.* I would say, maybe **pathologizing** a bit? or-

JB: Yeah*!* yeah*!*.

CB: -That works for his .. his *theory.* I looked up a word I should know by now, *a priori* .. you probably know that word; and apparently you start with the theory and then you .. you start with the what, *deduction,* and then you, prove it *later?*

JB: (*mutual laugh*)

CB: The way I just *naturally* prefer to work is: Start with a clinical material and then see what comes *out* of it.

-where with Freud here, we want to go *back* to the clinical material & see if it proves his point, or not.

JB: Right*!*

CB: So I think you've said a number of times,
what neurosis?
And then,
> *SF:* *"I was very glad to see him again,
> [because] for about two years after the end
> of his analysis I had lost sight of him and
> had heard nothing of him for more than 10
> years."*

CB: So we had to figure that out; it had been
about, a number of years; heard nothing.

Oh and then, *you* pointed this out,
> *What analysis?*

> *SF:* *"... about two years after the end of **his
> analysis** .. "*

-and I put that in quotes, "*analysis*" and I think
you were saying,
> What *analysis?* ~ What *lol* was the
analysis?

Do you have anything more to say on *that*
one?

JB: No it's just, it was the *father's* analysis wasn't it.

CB: Well the father was analyzing, supposedly little Hans. *Uh* he was a stand-in Analyst for -.

JB: -wasn't Freud analyzing the father at this time?

CB: Ohh well that *could be* too; they had a close relationship of some type. In fact I read somewhere, here's a new one, when- when Hans, or Herbert, was going to be circumcised - which is usually after 8 days - Freud was asked, 'well should I get him circumcised?' and he had said, 'well I guess you should because it will give him more- more of- of a *challenge* .. then, to deal with things..'   (slight lol)

JB: -Yeah that's a strange notion, isn't it?!

CB: yeah that's, maybe that's great coming a anti-circumcised point of view; at the same time, was Freud circumcised at 8 days old. And what about his family.. He had come from this Hasidic family but was already assimilated into Germany.

- but I get ahead of myself -

JB: -yeah I don't know the *answer* to that.

CB: So those are things to maybe check. But meanwhile - he's using the term, *'analysis'* - and our question was - *who* was doing an analysis? The father was supposedly standing-in as an analyst. You had asked before whether he analyzed anybody else?

Umm.. so - what analysis - is what you *were* saying ..

JB: um-hymm

CB: .. and ..

   SF: "..The publication of this first analysis of a child caused a great stir and ..."

And again, I think you had brought that up again. …
'Is that an analysis, really?

.. might be some other comments here too from the past .. but I think that's a good beginning*!* for people to think about ..

JB: R i g h t.   /   *CB:* .. -what analysis-

CB: -and then I had noticed at the very beginning .. in terms of the *next paragraph* and then I noticed something else, more recently. So tune in to the phrase, *"severest of ordeals."* And tune into the phrases that everything was fine [*"perfectly well"*]; he had *"come through"* so well.

And we read this paragraph. And yet, what about the **family** .. the family was totally torn apart, and Hans was out of touch now, with his sister. But from Freud's point of view - everything seemed to work well.

Okay so I'll read the paragraph and then we'll get back into all this.
Is everyone ready?

JB: Yep.   *CB:* Ok *lol*

CB:

SF: "But none of these apprehensions [that he spoke of in the paragraph JB just read], none of these apprehensions had come true. Little Hans was now a strapping youth of nineteen. He declared that he was perfectly well, and suffered from no troubles or inhibitions..*

CB: Sounds like a short conversation too.

SF: - "Not only had he come through his puberty with-out any damage, but his emotional life had successfully undergone one of the severest of ordeals.   - *CB:* Next line. -

His parents had been divorced and each of them had married again. In consequence of this he [Hans] lived by himself; but he was on good terms with both of his parents, and only regretted that as a result of the breaking-up of the family he had been separated from the younger sister he was so fond of."

CB: So, I already gave a kind of a Preview on this.

Here he's saying, 'everything worked out so well' .. "perfectly well' [as per Hans] .. "a *strapping youth"* - - he's just looking at his appearance. Apparently.

Uh and yet Freud also *acknowledges* that family dynamics are in the .. in the picture*!* - even though he pays little or no or scant attention to these things. *"..the **severest** of ordeals. His parents had been divorced.."*

JB: Right.

CB: And he's right. That is a severe ordeal. But that doesn't get into the Freudian *theory* very much at all ~

~ and then the public and the culture starts looking only within the negative aspects of the Consciousness ~ and doesn't look at these *outer* concerns, like, family ordeals.

JB: Well,I think the point here is: The early years .. the issues of the early years have been resolved, and so that he was able to face the divorce of his parents without being thrown by it; I think that's his point.

CB: Yeah that *is* his point, that's a good .. a good Summary of *his* point.

Now what do *you* think about his point?

JB: ... I think it makes sense ...

CB: .. well as far as it goes .. yeah.
 uh But at the same time he's saying that Hans was 'perfectly well.' *uh* and how long a conversation was this? -did he see him at a theater- *uh* he didn't have him back in therapy; and it sounds like it's pretty superficial conversation certainly the way he, portrays..doesn't get into much of anything ..

JB: -right. Yeah ..yeah - I think it was..

CB: ...so how can he say, that he came through it '*perfectly well*?'

What he *doesn't* say by the way is that part of the *split* between the mother and the father was: the mother - *and a lot of this I'm getting from internet sources so they can always be double check by any historian* - but that the mother, was no longer a Freudian. She moved over to the Alfred Adler point of view and the Alfred Adler approach .. such as *uh* **encouraging** children, in things that Freud never got into it all .. in fact Adler was much more into the politics of the times as well, but I think **encouragement** also meant a different type of relating to a child.

So there is a big split in.. in the field of .. the parents .. of baby Hans.

-so .. so your summary is accurate. What he's trying to say .. however what he's trying to say I don't think so supported…in any *detail.* Looks like half-a-paragraph or one.. one sentence. .. He just..

JB: .. well this is a.. just his superficial..*you know,* they just meet for a short time; this is an *impression* he has; I don't think he.. he claims anything deeper than that you know.

CB: Well he said he had "*successfully undergone*" one of the "*severest of ordeals*" .. I don't know that, and now he's separated from the younger sister he was so fond of. So to me as a family therapist that's a *potential failure ..* in it.

JB: .. well that wasn't a failure on *his* part.

CB: .. no, no, Freud doesn't involve himself in that ..

JB: .. no, I mean it wasn't a failure on *Hans'* part, that he was separated from his sister ..

CB: .. no, no, I'm not saying that.- I'm saying a failure of doing..therapy ..with a family ..is usually thought of .. *is* when the family deteriorates and breaks up ((sometimes not, sometimes it's necessary)) .

JB: .. I don't think this is seen as a .. family therapy .. is a more of a therapy of little Hans.

CB: .. Well that's, yeah, I know we have different points of view on that.

I think that's a ***Blind Spot*** of Freud's .. And *now* if Freud was only limited to a small group of clinical scientists who are only looking at what's going on in somebody's head ~ *Fine!*

However that's not what Freud has become.

He's thought of as the family .. *uh* as 'in the family' as like the "***father***" *of psychology* rather than as a ***pioneer***..someone lobbying on the part of his own point of view.. of a certain type of psychol-

JB: -well he's the father of Psycho*analysis* I think.

CB: Well he's the father, to me of *Freudian* ..psychoanalysis. And to me *uh you-know* I would say, more of a ***pioneer*** because there's a lot of ((even)) Freudians now who disagree with him.

But that's how he positioned himself - as the ***father*** of *psycho*analysis - which I say, that's not true; he's the father of ***Freudian***-defined, old-fashioned psychoanalysis.

Because he's <u>left</u> <u>out</u> a major, major portion of
the *Human Being*.

… …

JB: .. In .. in what way?

CB: Well the Human Being, from my research -
and from *yours* as a rabbi, has the yetzer Hara
and the yetzer Tov. How do you say it?

JB: Yetzer ha-*rah* and the yetzer ha-*tov*.

CB: And I think *that's* pretty accurate*!*
And my clinical work proves that it *is.*

I have 23 or 24 *((Initial))* cases .. of .. clinical
examples - of finding the *good part* of the
human being.

I mean I've done a lot of research in all the
pathology and all the *mishegas* and all the
negatives in the human beings' consciousness
.. but if you or if *he* is leaving out - the
strongest or at least the *best* and the most
urgently *required* part - and is only focusing on

all the *negatives* - - What shape does that
leave the, the world, in?

-What shape does that leave the psychological
climate or emotional climate in? if he's not
covering the *Ha-Tov* - the *good.* That wasn't
his *aim* as you'll say, *you-know* he didn't *aim* to
do that.

Yeah he was only looking at Pathology.
Supposedly.
But go ahead; what would you *say* to that..?

JB: That's where his focus was.

CB: That's exactly right. We agree on that.
   That's where his Focus *was.*

But what's urgently required *these* days - a
hundred years later and people are still…
those who don't really look at these details or
follow the details they still think of Freud as
the, the *progenitor* of psychological..research
into consciousness. -?-

JB: Well he made..he made.. He had *extraordinary insights* that were .. very helpful.
. . .

CB: Well to *who?*

JB: .. to *uh* the whole field of psychology. .. Of therapy.

CB: We can talk a little more on that, and we can talk about, was any of this helpful to Little Hans? Because when you go back over all the details of the rest of this book or this Audio, and hundred pages of notes, you see all these things very ..very clearly in terms of, nothing much applies - to little Hans.

I could remind you something ..does anything come to mind about that? such as *uh* …
thinking that the horse is his father because of the bridle. Because it is dark, and Freud thinks it reminds Hans of his father's moustache. So the horse must represent the father.
((can SEE: a graphic drawing of the above in Freud's book p 49))

Does that ring a bell?

JB: I didn't remember that, but it sounds a little bit far-fetched.

CB: Exactly*!* It's in there and you do say the same thing each time: "pretty far-fetched" or "pretty thin." So any of these details when we look at little Hans - which is pretty much the..the focus of this book.. (We're getting into these other areas a little bit as we conclude here.) .. but whenever we look into details, you see it as 'pretty thin' or 'not applying at all.'

You *have* seen it that way.

JB: W e l l. .. I .. I think there *are you-know* some insights that are helpful .. and I would say, It's a mixed bag.

CB: .. Well can you .. later or at any point, any reader or yourself or anybody can point out - which ones are the good .. which ones are helpful to little Hans?

JB: Well I think when we go over that earlier material, that we talk about that*!*

CB: Yeah, we do. We do. *(Smile)* ..and we don't find much of anything.. *Once in awhile* we find something that's interesting *um* or well-put, but I'd say 10 to 1 at least, these things are .. like you could not, he couldn't really convince us of the *"Oedipal complex"* when it came to Little Hans not even the *"Castration complex"* because the mother had said,

     'if you stop if don't stop playing with your penis, or widdler, we will call Doctor A and have it cut off.'
-Remember that one?

JB: *Yeah !!*   *CB:* *(lol)* *So . . .*

CB: *That's*, to me, the, the basis of the *"Castration complex."*

JB: Yeah*!* That was rough*!!*

CB: Yeah, y*eah!!* and they didn't even realize it was - again - that *that* was something to look into. They must have been very **naive**[5] back then - thinking *[it's okay]* to say *Anything* to a child - and it doesn't mean *anything* ..

.. well I think that'd be *real* rough. So if-

JB: *Umm!!* I agree. Yeah*!*

CB: -So if that's the Basis of the *Whole Concept* of the "Castration complex." And that's the best he could come up with.

Uh .. that's Disproven - - if we limit it to 'little Hans.'

If people want to look into other areas to try to prove it - *fine* - but little Hans is given a *lot* of focus. Even though it wasn't Freud's direct case, it's one .. I think *some say,* it's his most *famous* case.

.. so ..

---

[5] *Na·ive* /nīēv/ *Def.,* (of a person or action) showing a lack of experience, wisdom, or judgment.: "the rather naive young man had been totally misled".

Again these Concepts get going.. Some *[not just]* in the Jewish area know the term, '*Bubbameister*'[6] -?- I think, you know that one, right?

JB: S u r e.

CB: So .. *(and maybe I'll footnote that)* But how much of this becomes a *bubbameister* that gets - almost like a rumor - that is built upon.

 ((Bubbameister def., a long story or old wives' tale, that is, something a Grandma would tell. Yiddish, from "Bubba," "grandmother."))

Or as *[Norman]* Mailer used to say, a "*Factoid*" ~ Something that's written somewhere and they're not even looking at the details; now it's written in the newspapers; so now someone's quoting something *else;* and you're like a third-hand quote, and, people are not getting back to the *basic data* .. like *we're doing.*
 ((Check "Factoid" in Wikipedia or via our e-book))

---

[6] *Bubbameister* *def.*, a long story or old wives' tale, that is, something a Grandma would tell. *Yiddish*, from *"Bubba,"* "grandmother."

We *are looking* at this basic *data*.

So In terms of the *Castration complex,* how much of it do you think is a Bubbameister?

I know it's hard for you to *(little laugh)* answer that 'cause you are *very pro--Freud.* I want to ask you how come? but, you know, you're kind of like a *Believer,* of Freud, as like-a-father. And yet with the little Hans, you don't see it.

JB: ... yeah ... I- I don't see.. I don't see where this is very.. *illustrative*[7] of.. of *uh,* of his concepts.

CB: Yeah, well what do you think about like the "Castration complex" as a, as a complex (and then later I'll ask you, where did you first learn that?) but what do you think about the..just the concept of castration complex?

JB: ...I- have no feeling about it, positive or negative. I don't know..

---

[7] *Illustrative, <u>pronounced</u>. **Def.,** serving as an example or explanation.*
      [CB: a -great word- I do say!]

CB: ... yeah okay that's not a biggie. But I think when we've talked, neither one of us had any awareness *[personally]* of the castration *complex.*

JB: ...well I don't think he illustrates it very well- In this case, you know.

CB: No, I totally agree. In that. ~ *Umm .. so uh ..*

JB: ...whether that means that they - it's a valid or invalid - hard to say, but it's a poor .. This is a poor example of it I think.

CB: *Amen.* ~ On that one.

So, what about the *"Oedipal complex"* [*a.k.a. the Oedipus Complex*]" ? - Because we do cover that a little bit, when he's trying to say that Hans wants to have sex with the mother and kill the father, replace the father.

And neither one of us really - again - won't see the *support* in that. And we do cover that a little bit..

JB: -yeah, I think that uh- well certainly the idea of him sleeping- of little Hans staying with the mother.. and the father not being with her, was very satisfying to him.

CB: .. was satisfying to .. ?

JB: - little Hans.

CB: ...*was* satisfying?

JB: Yeah.

CB: ...well we both were saying..

JB: ... *Alone* with his mother in bed.

CB: Well, we were.. I don't know about *that*.. but we were saying, "Sleeping with" to you and to me, meant "sleeping with." Didn't mean sex.

JB: … No, no.   CB: (*slight laugh*) …

CB: He just wanted the *affection* of having his mother close and when she's traveling or something, he was.. disturbed, by that..

JB: Right.

CB: .. but he even brought his father into his play-time, *uh* n' said, *'you can be the* grand-pappy *(of these little dolls) and I'll be the father (of the* dolls).' And how much of *that* even got going ..from their *own* discussion.. I don't *know..* how much was put into his head..

But even *there* he wasn't trying to *eliminate* his father.

So, do you think that's a pretty valid concept though, the *Oedipal?*

JB: Oh, *Yeah!* ~ But I don't think it's well-Illustrated with little Hans.

CB: no; right ... So - Where did you first learn about it & why do you think it's valid?

I mean, you were saying in the past that, there's *Rivalry* and I was.. my response, earlier in this book was - Yeah there's *Rivalry* all over the place - It's not just father~son. .. It's sister~brother; It's mother and father ~ their rivalry ~ sometimes between each ,,

Um but in general, what.. what do you think about the "*Oedipal complex?*"

In general, is it mostly *Rivalry* that you're talkin' about?

JB: Yeah I think so, yeah.

CB: . . . .
 'cause to me, that's *rivalry* if it's.. If it comes to the point of.. of killing and life and death - - that's very Capital **R** - - *Rivalry.* I mean that's a big, big deal; that's pretty *pathological* when it.. when it gets out-of-hand like that*!*

'cause what about *Normal* rivalry vs. *Pathological* rivalry .. ?
. . . Any thoughts on *that* one?

JB: Oh.. I- I think it's.. probably that there's jealousy for the.. possession of the mother, but *you know,* it's uh .. I don't think it's a *major ..* or it's a *crippling* thing; I just think that.. I think it's part of.. the *normal..development* of the.. the child.

CB: Well I think, yeah.. I would agree.. could be.. Should be *"normal.."* especially..   . I think it comes largely from the attitude of the family, *you know* the culture, of the many generations and particularly of the mother and of the father.

If they think of.. *lets say,* the wife as being under the *possession of* the father -as it *was* probably in the 1900s, more.. before Women's Lib- And then the father becomes jealous and the son becomes jealous, and they're competing *"all over the damn place"* ..

Then *that's* part of the *problem*. And then, the *more severe* that *gets* the *worse* it can become.

-whether it's father-*son*, whether it's sister-brother.. It's really a lack of *Balance*. And a lack of *let's say Fair-play*, and a lack of *um* I would say, *Integration*.[8]

*((SEE: **Psychointegration**.com - 1st in 2012 **CB**-defined, video w/ Distracting sounds!!))*

It's more **ego**-defined[9] rather than **id**-defined. It's more *developed* instead of *primitive*. And it's not just the Yatza *Hora* where it's the negative impulse, but it's also the Yeytzer *Tov* where there's *balance*.
((*"Ego"* in a Freudian or general Clinical sense; *not "Big Ego"* as per A.A. or in a Colloquial sense.))

Then there's not going to be a severe Oedipal *thing* at *all*.
    -What do *you* think- .. on *that* one.

---

[8] *Psychointegration* Initially, *2012 as CB-defined*..more forthcoming..*(1st)* w/ Distracting sounds!!

[9] *"Ego" in a Freudian or a general Clinical sense. Not "Big Ego" as per A.A. or colloquial sense.*

JB: Well I think it's a ***natural*** thing that there should be.., that the Rivalry is *natural* .. It's not .. *you-know* I think it can *get pathological,* become something that's *overwhelming* and interferes with the child's development; that's, that's obviously a *problem..*

CB: Right.

JB: -well I think it's probably the *normal development of the child*.

CB: Now what about *let's say,* between sister and brother..*uh* is that normal?

JB: -I don't think to the same extent.
　　　. . .

CB: -how.. why do you *think* that?
　　　. . .

JB: -just Seems to me that there is A child's possession of the mother, and the father interfering with that.. that seems to me to be a source of *uh* concern.

CB: -well hope.. hopefully the father Would be more mature. Let's say the sister and brother are 10 and 12 Years old or something, so neither one is mature but When the father is involved - if he's mature - And where are things, he's going to be more *uh* In the process; he's going to be more *mindful* of what's going *o-n*.

JB: -Oh yeah, I think, To the extent that the father is *aware* of this… I think that will work much better than if he's **blind** to it.

CB: Now do you think Freud focused almost *primarily* on *this*, and left out.. What's going on with the sisters in the brothers. Let's say, a brother and a sister as I say. 10 and 12 years old .. Then you have two people fighting for the mother Who are pretty, most likely, *immature* - Compared to a 25 or 35 year old- ..father -

JB: -I think this is when a child is *younger* than 10 or 12. I think this probably when the.. This is the first couple of *years- !*

CB: -Okay, when the child is *two* and the other child is *four* ..If it's handled *improperly..*

JB: -I'm talking about the, *uh* when the child is *two* .. And the business with the *mother,* you know*..*

CB: -Well yeah let's say the two.. the two young babies are fighting over the mother And the mother is not aware of that ... Is not into how to *Soothe* them, how to Keep them *balanced ... uh* How to *uh* soothe the situation but she *inflames* the situation ... And *highlights* the *competition ..*

That can get pretty *rough; I would say* logically, it can be even *rougher than-*

JB: -I'm not talking about the competition between the *siblings;* I'm talking about The

competition between the *child* and the *father!*
The male-   */// - C l i c k -*

CB: *W o o p s ! ! !   Did you just get cut out? …
(laughing) -* I heard a *C-l-i-ck*, and I don't know
if you can still *hear* me … ?

But just *my* part of this, the Conclu- ///
Beep~boop~Beep~boop~Beep

Oh. ~ That's what happens with that phone ..
Kind of - - cuts out.   . . .
But, just to Conclude this, and I guess I'm
given the *"lucky break"* here of .. of *lol.. j*ust me
concluding it .. And that is:

If you have a 2 year old and a 4 year old, That
can get pretty, *Intense!* And then you don't
have anyone balancing it out. And then if the
mother's in there Stirring up the pot - - That's
going to be more *intense* than let's say a two
year old boy with his 25-year-old father .. *If* the
father is *balanced.*

And these are the things that dear Freud, Sigismund anyway, did *not* pay attention to. Did not pay really.. *any..* attention to.

And I think it- I'm sure I'm not the *only one* who's saying this. But again it brings up the idea that- ((..and I *might* be.)) But it brings up the idea of ***Blind Spots,*** of Freud.

-Which wouldn't be so *urgent* a hundred years later, except for the fact that people still *follow him* as "*having-the-last-word.*"

I look at him as having the *first-word* about a number of things or, early in the field, but not the *last*-word by any means. And look at Anna Freud as an example; she looked much more at the *Family; uh* she looked at the *Self* and my- /// *R~I~N~G Dial Tone* /// -my- // - *R i n g* - // -*hypothesis* is .. (& I'll shut that down) .. *"Hang up or call your Operator"*

- That some of the *followers* of Freud .. noticed some of the *decrements,* things missing.. And added them in.

Freud's daughter, Anna, noticed these a lot, and she wrote about the *Self* - And she takes a look at things in a.. in a very different *way.*

So. Okay; have I stopped *recording*? No not quite.

So in Conclusion of that Postscript. The Third Paragraph.
It says,
*"One piece of information given me by little Hans struck out, or struck me as particularly remarkable .." // Tel. Answering Ring !! //
((Whoops - what happened here Oh! it switched over to another phone))*

CB: Okay, you're back on.. the end of the *recording!*

JB: - Y a h. -

CB: And I.. just want to cover.. that *last* paragraph, real briefly.

JB: - O.K. -

CB:

SF: "One piece of information given me by little Hans struck me *as particularly remarkable.*"

And then my comment was, I had put, *Really* ?

And then when you really read through this, I don't think anything's *"remarkable."* At all in this.

And then there's also a footnote, at the end, about this phenomenon of not remembering things when you wake up - That you're dreaming and when you wake up you don't remember them.

I'm not sure how remarkable that is; and in fact I'm sure that's totally *un*remarkable,

JB: Oh yeah*!*, Sure*!*   *(CB laugh)*

CB: Even by the standards of the 1800s, they *dreamt* I'm sure.. And someone must have realized, 'I don't *remember* it when I wake up*!*'

JB: Oh, yah*!*

CB: So he's making this into *'remarkable'* and to me it's kind of.. almost a diversionary.. paragraph. It puts the tension where it doesn't need to be.

And then there's a footnote below *that,* that there was something added to his *Interpretation of Dreams* - in 1911*!* - so that doesn't really prove the point *here.*

And again, is it *remarkable?*

JB: I think not, *no.*   (*CB laugh*)

CB: So, we'll conclude on *that* one, I guess. -and I don't know if we *uh,* do we assume that *uh,* the telephone system *uh,* run by the One Above, cut into our conversation a little bit there?

JB: I think that this *charges up,* and uses a certain amount of electricity and just quits.. *CB:* yeah, yeah we've seen that over a long period.. of time & I keep saying, *what about getting a new uh, a new phone* ..*JB: (laughing)* & *CB: (laughing).*

JB: I'm *used* (laughing) to this one*! -* I don't..I don't get *anything* (lol) new*!*

CB: (laughing). 'cause in.. -Or a *New Freud* for that matter*! Lol & a laugh*

But in the kitchen it's a beautiful *rotary dial;* one of our cousins actually put it up on the internet, a picture of a rotary-dial-phone in the kitchen. But that's the most stable one of all*!*

JB: Yeah, right*! ..lol*   *CB:* Never breaks .. *!*

JB: That's true of *most* old-fashioned things*! Better* than the *replacements!*

CB: -so you *might* want to.. think again of getting a landline phone in the study and then.. with the *option* of a battery pick-up .. saying I had two that gave out but I'm still using the base.. In fact this landline phone is still working; it's just that the other, extra equipment..already *gave out.*

CB: So maybe there are some *parallels* here.. with what we're talking about.

~you like, the *Basic Freud* ~ before it was kind of.. updated a bit, *like say Contemporary analysis..* but I wanted to ask you, *Where did you learn that?* was that from your *own analysis* of three years *[plus]* -

JB: I think probably I studied it in *school..* Psychology classes I *would think.*

CB: Yeah, you were saying something about- ..attitudes about hypnosis -

JB: I was a psychology major *y'know* in college so-

CB: So this was undergraduate-   *JB:*   -I learned it there, yah .

CB: guess what? So was I -- sociology and psychology. I had to change from..mathematics .. get back to what I . really wanted to *do.*

So, you had learned about at the time, that Hypnosis was dangerous; I had learned that

Hypnosis had a lot of promise. 'Cause mine was in the year 1962 *I would think*, and yours was in the year *1942,* maybe?

-your "Introduction to Psychology"…? ..

JB: .. ahh…. let's see, I would have been... I think I was around 16

CB: So this does prove *one* thing related to Freud … if you, if we extrapolate from *"Early Childhood experiences."* These are *"Early Psychology experiences."*

And they leave *an effect!*

We all get into Advanced work, Graduate school, but we *forget* our very *early Introductions.*

And was your introductory teacher a Freudian *advocate,* and he really *strongly* felt that Freud was the Father of all of Psychology, or what were his attitudes, do you remember?

JB: No-o I don't remember but I think that was just the generally Accepted View.

CB: Maybe was that the *only* accepted view .. *wasn't it -?-*

JB: Yeah, pretty much.

CB: -other than *[B.F.] Skinner* or some *Behavioral* things coming up *later-?*

JB: Yeah there was *Skinner* but this was.. this was Freud's big contribution.

CB: *-Yeah-* Everyone *admired* him ... Interesting- *JB: Umm-hym.*

CB: -Interestingly enough, I think he had a lot of entitlement and narcissism because his mother admired him to a *fault!*

She said, " That's my *golden Sigmund!* "

There was no question that he was elevated beyond *all* the other siblings. - - And Freud thought that was *great.* He writes about that. 'You can do no wrong when your mom, your mama, thinks of you on such a high level ~ *especially* above all your siblings.'

I was looking to see if he did any *discussion* of that as a *Pathology (LOL).* I couldn't find anything, so far.   ...

JB: -well it was mostly Psychology.. *y'know* the.. the whole world of *psychology..* responded in many cases very *positively..*   *CB:* -well yeah.

JB: -and he spoke with a *Prophetic voice you know.*

CB: -oh, I didn't know, ..a *prophetic voice?*

JB: Prophetic. Yeah.

CB: -Well he *was* prophetic because World War II came out of that, the *uh* destruction of half the Jewish people *um* and all sorts of *horrible things.* So it was prophetic, in the

terms of looking at the *Pathology.*   (...and..& I
sure hope it wasn't one of the *factors..)*

But it was *prophetic!*
I'd agree on.. on *that.*

-but my point was, the Mama looked upon him
so positively, that when he started working in
the field of psychology and in the climate of
Germany at the time *um* and in the World-at-
Large -as well as his family- *that* rubs off*!*

And then that's like a very basic *thing* to most
people - what the parent or parents *think* of
them*!* so if this mother thought *so highly* of
him-
  JB: -Yah!   *CB: .. how* could he go wrong?

JB: Well, most Jewish mothers feel that.

CB: (laugh) What happened to mine*?* -or maybe
she- / -hid it well ..

*JB: (laughter) / -*I said, *m*ost not *all* of them. *(Lol*
)

CB: -okay *(Lol)* I heard the "*most*" in there. JB: *(lol)* - - /

CB: / -Actually- *(softly)* I think she *did* think pretty well of me when I was very young [& thereafter tho *hidden* a bit] so maybe there *is* something there.

CB: *Fortunately* there is something *deeper* than Freud's *contributions*. I think it's deeper. It's certainly *better,* and it's not the *Pathology*; it's the *Health*.

It's the Yetzer *Tov* as compared to the Yetzer *Ha-Rah*.
Ha-Rah and *horrible* issues that can occur in.. in the *destructive* side of people.

So he was very helpful in *that* - to say, well, 'let's look at the *destruction* and what *that's* all about.'

But how do you *fix* that? ..and that is- / JB: Psyc- / CB: I.. I believe-

JB: Psycho-analysis*!*

CB: Well how does psychoanalysis *fix* that.. *?*

JB: -well you establish a *relationship* between the An[-alyst & patient] *{-sound cut out-}* .. the role of a father; and you sort of *relive* those earl..early experiences*!*

CB: Well that's what he says ~ and I'm not *sure* that's true even in *analysis* ~ but what's the *Outside* of analysis, where the *struggle* is with the *millions* of people instead of the *thousands* of people who are *in* *psychoanalysis* or *were;* and the struggle is in the whole *culture* and the *climate.*

-how do you *fix that*? They're not looking at Freud in *depth* the way *we are*. They're assuming that these assumptions, he's sharing, are *true* -

- and that just allows *continued* destruction, War, pestilence, and *uh* pissiness, and all the stuff that happens out there. It doesn't help get *Beyond* it for the people in general.

-and again I'll just come back one more time; I don't want to talk this to death 'cuz I want to talk it to *life* ~ Where does the Yetzer *Tov* fit into this?

The Good Stuff - - that's what *I've* researched. And now have researched for a good *twenty-five years,* the 'Yetzer Tov'..
/ *JB:* -*WELL*- / ..in the *person.*

JB: -*YEAH*- I think there- I think there's a *recognition* that there's.. certain.. positive reactions on the part of the child.
/ *CB:* -*Well* .. /

JB: - It's not *All* negative, you know.

CB: Well where's the theory? Where is the theory, any Freudian theory, that is talking about the Good side; and how to *reach* the good sides - - and that they're even *there;* I think Carl Jung might have *uh* touched on it a bit.

JB: I think the assumption that th- that their there; at all.. childhood.. there's more to the child then the *neuroses.*

CB: Well we hope so*!*

JB: … child feels .. *{Sound didn't come through}* for his parents ...

CB: Well I don't ..disagree with you. I don't disagree totally with that; I'm sure that there *might* be that assumption there; it's just that that wasn't where the *research* was. That wasn't where the *focus* was. There's an assumption..

JB: … well he was dealing with *Pathology.*

CB: Yeah. - that's my *point.* *JB:* -Yeah. ..well he wasn't dealing with *normal relationships.*

CB: well what about-? What's the opposite of *Pathology* would you say?

JB: Health*!*

- - -

CB: Health-ology! (Mutual laugh) And that's..

That's what *"The Still Soft Voice"* is about.

Now you have that book of mine, right?

JB: Right.

CB: .. and you agreed with me that we *will* go over Chapter *One .. ?!*
Does that ring a bell?   *JB: Sure, ..*

JB: … but you know.. but you know that-
{Sound didn't come through} -positive feeling about the *hypnosis ..?..* so you have to deal with *that .. you know.*

CB: Oh I'll deal with that..   *JB: Yeah.*   *CB:* I'll deal with that, first of all because I *know how that goes* 'cuz we *have* dealt with that & it is.. it is in our e-book.

About the *Changes* in hypnosis, and, it's being accepted by all sorts of Societies .. but more than that I don't do *hypnosis exactly.*

I do something almost the *opposite* of hypnosis; I'm making that clear to the Psychoanalytic Institute folks .. that I don't do *standard* hypnotherapy even the "*best*" type - which is good- a *non*-Authoritarian hypnosis, I think *is* a better type or the *best* type*!*

But I took it a step further: I only use that *process* To go in deep into the consciousness - To see what's naturally *there!* ..

And for 20 or 40 years, I was pretty good at getting into the *Negatives* .. Find out, *what's the Problem* . and how to *fix that*. So I do agree that it's *there* [*the negatives*].

The *New Part* of what I do is how to get people *out* of Trance, *out* of hypnosis and *find that inner voice* ~ that inner *excellent* voice, that *Still Soft Voice.*

There *are* some *concerns* I have about ((Authoritarian hypnosis)) in the World-at-large or in the Family when the family is *Authoritarian* or the Politician or leader of the country is *authoritarian,* it leads to great evil - - and that's a Negative hypnosis.

And that leads to destruction, so I would agree with your instructor on that *part* of it but I'm just saying, that also has led to some very great breakthroughs about the still soft voice, the inner core..

Okay. Anything in conclusion here? .. First of all-

JB: I think the Inner Core.. I think that the idea that.. the child has. very positive *uh* impulses as well as the negative, you know that's- I think that's *true.*

CB: Well thank you, okay ~ because I think *Freud's* view of the inner core is very different from *my* view of the inner core. I'd say there's maybe *two* inner cores but which one is the..the *dominant?*

I think.. *(Well)* you know what I think *(laugh)*.. - -

JB: When the neurosis is *removed,* then the *other* is dominant.

CB: Well how are we *doing* in the world these days..*?*
  JB: hymm?   CB: How's the *world* doing these days with that*?*

JB: Well I think you have *both you-know* ..where.. have people who are deeply neurotic; and you have people who are less so.

CB: Well I.. I hear what you're saying because I know where the original, early Freudians were *at. "Make the unconscious conscious,"* it all works out, and people will just work it out for themselves. Now *really* that's a very *positive* statement when you think about it*!*

If it's true ~ that you don't have to help the person find the *good;* you just have to help the person find the bad; and then the good comes out by itself.

Well that's- that's *positive;* I like that concept. If only it were true. It's not true but if it were true, that would be *wonderful.* Then I'd agree with it*!*

So I've- I've always said that hidden away in Freud, are some very *ah* mystical, positive, even Jewish, Yiddish, concepts*!* -Hasidic*!* .. don't forget his parents were both *Hasidic* .. but .. *he* got away from that, and *they* got away from that, but their real positive stuff probably rubbed off on him, somewhere. Hopefully.

Well o-kay. I know we can talk about this for another 30 years, since *(LOL)* we *have* been talking about it, for a long time. And we're.. coming up to almost 50 minutes; I don't know how I'm going to ever *transcribe* all this *(mutual laughter)* ..but I'll try to get the *basics / JB: Okay .. (LOL) /* for the e-book, and then those people who want the *whole thing,* they can have- They

can hear all of it. *JB: Hym-hym!*   *CB:* If that's
okay with *you..*

JB: Sure!

CB: Okay, with me too.
So *thanks for listening* if you're still with us- out
there..*!*

JB: Okay!

CB: I meant to the people listening - but *you too!*
So I'll stop the recording at this point, and hope
that, we captured it.

It's been a *good discussion.*

JB: Oh yeah!

CB: -About Little Hans .. and .. Way Beyond-

JB: (LOL) ..

CB: .. As you said .. a *"Post post-Postscript."*

Freud's Fallacy

~

169

www.ingramcontent.com/pod-product-compliance
Lightning Source LLC
Chambersburg PA
CBHW031115250726

48655CB00004B/1724